I Pledge Allegiance:
A Veteran's Dream

Annie Amerika

Every day is a good day to be green!

~Annie Amerika 2/2015

ISBN: 1480023264
ISBN-13: 978-1480023260

Cover photo courtesy of Carrie Draeger, *Lake Chelan Mirror*

DEDICATION

This book is dedicated to the love of my life,
my husband John.

He taught me how to love my country
and to be a proud patriot.

With all my heart I will love you forever...

ACKNOWLEDGEMENTS

I'd like to thank the many people and patriotic groups that supported me as I set out to make this patriotic journey a reality.

A special thank you goes out to VFW #6853 Chelan, WA and Michael Harris for being the first to believe in and support me on my excursion, thank you for allowing John to be Jr. Vice Commander in your fine group of dedicated men and women.

To Teresa Nelson for being my friend, you were always there to laugh and cry with me. Your friendship has been true to me for over 30 years.

Thank you to Jennifer Marshall Best, the first person to interview me. She also wrote weekly updates in our local paper keeping our community up to date on my patriotic tour of our country. You were my editor and without your patience and expertise this book may have never made it to publication.

I also want to acknowledge the support and love from my family Eric and Sara, Joe and Lindsay, Sierra and Brett, my seesters Maureen and Elizabeth and my daddy Ken. Family is forever!

To the patriotic people I gave flags to across our magnificent country, your stories have forever changed my life, and I thank you from the bottom of my heart.

1
THE STORY OF US

John and I met in South Lake Tahoe, California, in September of 1980. Our relationship was one that never should have happened; our love was almost instant, and you could call it magic. Within a month of meeting we were talking about our future together. John even asked, "If we ever have a daughter, can we call her Sierra?" My answer was yes! What a beautiful name and a beautiful place we lived, the Sierra Nevada Mountains. Our life was not easy in the early months, but our love was strong. I was 23 years old and he was 32. We were soul mates.

We also had what I like to call the "white picket fence" - even though we never had an actual white picket fence, we did have a full circle relationship. We were together for five years before our children were born. We raised and nurtured them until they left home after graduation from high school. Our son, Joe, went to college and our daughter, Sierra, became a resident at a fire station. Then we had another five years together, until his death.

Since we had almost five years together before our first child was born, we talked about many things. John told me about his love for his country and how he and his best friend, Colin, enlisted in the Navy together. They had heard that if you enlist instead of being drafted, you can choose what you want to do, they were wrong. Both of them were proud to be in the Navy and serving their country. John spoke little of his time in Vietnam, but he did tell me about the treatment he received when he got home to the states, and it was not good. This is probably why he marched in just about any parade he could, proudly wearing his military green shirt and his arrangement of pins and badges. He always talked about his love for our country and his patriotism to our American flag.

When John died, we had been together for thirty years. My world fell apart. I look back on it now and realize I was in a state of shock for weeks after his death, maybe even months. I remember clearly the third day after his accident and I wasn't able to breathe. I had to force air into my lungs. You would think that breathing is automatic, something the body does by itself - except when you're in a state of shock.

The year following his death was a time of major decisions for me, and each of these adjustments brought forth excruciating pain because I miss him so very much. These are the reasons why I decided to complete John's mission: to honor his patriotism and his love for our country while trying to heal my heart. John genuinely is the love of my life, and I do realize just how blessed I was.

To John on our 25th wedding anniversary
When we met I was 23 you were 32;
Our life was wild and free,
Just you and me.
We married and made beautiful babies;
Our life was no longer wild and free,
But you were still 32 to me.
With our children grown and gone
We try to be wild and free.
Our bodies have aged, hairs of gray;
Skin visibly aged by our life of being wild and free.
And still
When I look into your eyes
You're still 32 to me!

25th wedding anniversary
Photo by Bre'Bee Photography

2

PREPARING

These logs were taken from my Facebook page and blog, where I chronicled my journey for hundreds of readers. Some of their comments are included here, with last names removed.

November 27, 2011

In the summer of 2010 my husband John - a disabled Vietnam veteran - and I planned at trip across America. We would visit long lost family members, national parks and the Vietnam Memorial Wall, and along the way we would replace old and tattered American flags for free. In the 30 years John and I were together, we noticed many tattered flags flying and wanted to take pride in replacing them with new flags. We also talked about donating the retired flags to local Boy Scout troops so they could learn how to properly retire them. We sold our 1979 Ford camper van and bought a classic Superior motor home. We named it Ginger in preparation for this once in a lifetime trip.

John was the most patriotic man I have ever met - he was proud to be an American and served in the Navy. On November 7, 2010, John was tragically killed in a single vehicle accident, and my life was turned upside down. I had to sell Ginger and the hopes of traveling across America with the man I love.

As time went on, I realized that this trip was extremely important to me, as it was to John. I bought a 1985 Chevy camper van and started planning my trip for the summer of 2012. My tentative plan is to leave North Central Washington on June 12, 2012 and return in mid-August. I am proud to be an American and proud to have loved such a patriotic man. Please follow along with me as I plan the endeavor and carry it out our dream.

John's beloved 1976 FLH Harley.

November 27, 2011

I was given the nickname Annie at a biker rally in Waterville, Washington in June 2011. Kids to the Capitol is a fundraiser motorcycle rally to send local kids to Washington, D.C. in the spring of 2013.

I arrived on Friday in the late afternoon and was quickly invited to join Kimberly and her husband, Gary, and their friends. Gary asked me my name and I said Gale. He quickly said, "I'll never remember that," and asked what my middle name is. I told him it was Ann, but I wouldn't acknowledge it because I have never been called Ann.

The next day I heard some loud, obnoxious voice yell across the fairgrounds, "ANNIE!" I turned and looked, along with about 20 other people, and Gary pointed to me and said, "That's it. From now on, your name is Annie." I argued for a while, but finally realized I would always be Annie to him. As the days and weeks went by I realized that Annie is a good, all-American name, so I embraced it and decided to use it for my trip.

January 2, 2012

The plan so far has me covering 8,602 miles going through Washington, Idaho, Montana, Wyoming, South Dakota, Minnesota, Wisconsin, Illinois, Indiana, Ohio, Pennsylvania, Maryland, West Virginia, Virginia, North Carolina, Tennessee, Alabama, Mississippi, Arkansas, Oklahoma, New Mexico, Colorado, Utah, Nevada, California, and Oregon, and then back to Washington.

January 14, 2012

Check out my new blog.
http://www.AnnieAmerika2012.blogspot.com

February 5, 2012

Thank you, Signs Etcetera!

I sent out many sponsor letters to different agencies. All major sponsors rejected me - oil companies, and national and recreational vehicle resorts. Locally owned Signs Etcetera of Waterville, Washington, was the first to respond with a "yes."

February 10, 2012

On Tuesday, February 21, I will be giving a presentation at the Lake Chelan Eagles Auxiliary. I am so excited to share my plans with them.

February 12, 2012

VFW Lake Chelan Post 6853 donated for the purchase of American flags!

Originally, I wasn't going to ask anyone for help with this trip. I wanted to quietly go in and replace flags without notice, but I also knew that when some of the organizations that John belonged to found out about this patriotic journey, they would have been disappointed if I hadn't contacted them. It was only fitting that I ask Lake Chelan Veterans of Foreign Wars to participate in this journey of a lifetime.

John was Jr. Vice Commander for the VFW in Lake Chelan. He has been a lifetime VFW member since the mid-1980s. Lake Chelan VFW Post No. 6853 was the first organization to donate for flags.

My first sponsor!

February 20, 2012

Tomorrow evening I will be presenting at the Lake Chelan Eagles and asking them to donate for the purchase of American flags. I am very excited!

John was an Eagles member in Lake Chelan. While at the FOE Auxiliary meeting I met Chris, and she told me to get in touch with her husband, Lynn. She said he, too, is a disabled Vietnam veteran and would be interested in my story. I contacted Lynn and he invited me to tell my story at the Chelan Sidecar Rally in May.

February 22, 2012

I want to thank Lake Chelan Ladies Auxiliaries to the local Aeries of The Fraternal Order of Eagles for allowing me to present to you last night my "Flags for America" event that I am undertaking this summer as Annie Amerika. The donation is to be used for the purchase of American flags. Thank you! I hope all of you can follow along on my journey through this blog.

Comments

Joyce: Thank you for the wonderful presentation! Lake Chelan Eagles Auxiliary supports you. And hope many others will support this very worthy cause!

David: My heart goes out to you. Your loss is America's loss sounds like your husband John was a

Great American. Your carrying out his dream will keep him alive forever! We need more Americans like you. At 15 yrs. old I spent a lot of time at the VFW & DAV hall talking with WWI WWII Korea & Vietnam vets I always gave them respect and shook their hand and thanked them for keeping America free every one of them were most grateful to serve their country. I was drafted during the Ted Offensive but because of a birth defect never went I was born with one kidney. But I went to the veterans Hospital and visited with our wounded vet. I served in my own way and still do I cry for them when I hear I am proud to be an American by Lee Greenwood. Sorry I was long winded, my love for my country runs deep.

March 1, 2012

Two more sponsor letters went out today. Hello, Big River RV Park and Jerry's Auto.

March 6, 2012

I ordered 30 outdoor American flags this morning. American made; stitched, not printed!

I ordered the flags from The Flag Store in Sparks, Nevada. John and I always bought our flags from them, so I thought it was fitting to order from them for my trip. At every home John and I owned or rented, he put up a flagpole, usually within the first week.

March 6, 2012

I received a hand-written note in the mail today with a donation for my trip, along with a $2 bill from a woman named Hope. She told me she met John once and "enjoyed being around him - who enjoyed music as well as being

'Superman' who could do 'any' thing!" She stated that the $2 bill was a lucky bill to be tucked into my wallet and not to be spent unless I'm broke. It's a tradition in her family to give a $2 bill to someone who has been kind to others or has a worthy project. I did tuck the $2 bill into my van and enjoyed the good luck.

March 14, 2012

Nice talk with Martin Smith at the Flag Store in Sparks, Nevada. When I called Martin and told him about my trip he agreed to give me a discount on all of my flags. Thank you, Martin!

I was at Nell's Café in Bridgeport talking to the owner, Nancine, about my summer plans and within moments she was on the phone with the *Quad City Herald*. And before I knew it, Jennifer was on the phone setting up an interview. Jennifer Marshall did an awesome job with this, my first article; she also did weekly follow up articles that I didn't know about until the last day of my journey.

March 14, 2012

My First newspaper article appeared in the Quad City Herald (see chapter 5). Until this first article was published, I had not wanted to reveal my true identity. I wanted to go into towns and replace tattered flags with homeowners' permission, but I did not want credit for it. After all, this trip is not about me - it is about John, his patriotism and my need to complete his wishes. I wanted to be like Santa Claus and just come in quickly and back out again. I did not want people to know my true identity or where I lived.

Jennifer convinced me that readers will want to know that there is really a person behind the moniker Annie Amerika.

March 14, 2012
  Thank you, Big River RV Park, for your sponsorship in "Flags for America."

Comments
  Victoria: We are so proud of you and what you are doing! Good-luck on your adventure! You will be in our prayers!

March 21, 2012
Lake Chelan Mirror newspaper article by Mike Torres appeared today. Thank you, Mike, and everyone at Lake Chelan Senior Center. When we moved to Lake Chelan in the summer of 2010, John quickly joined the Lake Chelan Senior Center and became involved in helping with the new thrift store in Chelan Falls.

March 28, 2012
  Thank you American Legion No. 54 of Chewelah, Washington, for your support!

March 31, 2012

Please support those who support me.

Thank you, Kimberly!

Signs Etcetera

I first met Kimberly at Kids to the Capitol fundraiser; who would have known she is a generous graphic artist? On my "Flags for America" journey, I received more compliments about the graphics on my van. I told everyone about the wonderful Kimberly at Signs Etcetera.

March 31, 2012

Annin American Flags have been American made since 1847. It was an Annin flag that flew at the inauguration of President Zachary Taylor, starting an inaugural tradition that has continued through the inauguration of President George W. Bush.

April 3, 2012

Thank you, Jerry's Auto & Truck Repair.

I had major concerns that my 1985 Chevy van with 110,000 miles on it wouldn't make a trip of this magnitude without some major work. Jerry gave my van a super tune up and included draining the transmission and putting in a new filter! He is an excellent mechanic and was very generous. Thank you, Jerry!

April 4, 2012

Big thanks to ITD Productions for your generous support. Please support those who support me.

On April 5 I received in the mail a gift from my friend, Carlen. I was thrilled to find this patriotic jacket. It will be my "forever" jacket. Thank you, Carlen!

April 16, 2012

Major sponsors: Please support those who support me, and in no special order.

- ITDProductions.com

- American Legion Columbia Post No. 97, Brewster, WA
- Lake Chelan Senior Center
- Veterans of Foreign Wars Post No. 6853, Lake Chelan, WA
- Lake Chelan Eagles Auxiliary No. 2218
- American Legion No. 54, Chewelah, WA
- Jerry's Auto & Truck Repair, Valley, WA
- Big River RV Park, Bridgeport, WA
- Signs Etcetera, Waterville, WA
- Bob Marley
- Flag Store, Sparks, NV
- Nell's Café, Bridgeport, WA
- Springer Tech, King City, OR
- CSR Chelan Sidecar Rally
- American Legion No. 108, Manson, WA
- Veterans of Foreign Wars Post No. 3617, East Wenatchee, WA

Comments

Carol: I am so proud of your efforts. What you are doing is so wonderful, and a special thank you to everyone that is helping support this project!

Maureen: Bob Marley?

April 17, 2012

I received another flag order; I now have 60 - 3x5, 6 - 4x6 and 1 -5x8. I'm still taking donations for what will probably be my last order.

Comments

Joyce: Lake Chelan Auxiliary 2218 is proud to be one of your many sponsors. Keep up the good work Sister!!!

April 20, 2012

My name is Gale Wilkison. I live in North Central Washington.

My husband John, a disabled Vietnam veteran, was killed in a single vehicle accident on November 7, 2010. The summer before he died we talked about sojourning across the country, visiting national parks and family. Along the way John wanted to replace worn and tattered American flags. The flags would be a free gift to the homeowner.

This summer I will embark on a cross country journey of America, replacing worn flags to honor my husband, our country and its veterans, and to help heal my heart. I will be using the name Annie Amerika as I spread patriotism throughout our great country. I'm leaving on June 10, 2012, traveling 60 days through 27 states and almost 9,000 miles.

I am asking everyone who reads this to follow along with me and my travels at www.AnnieAmerika2012.blogspot.com or at www.facebook.com/AnnieAmerika2012.

Comments

Lise: We'll be there, right beside you ALL the way.

Taegen: I know many people and places across our great country. Let me know if you want some travel tips or people tips. What an awesome trip.

Teresa: Annie Amerika 2012 bumper stickers are in the Mail.

Carol: I have the utmost respect and praise for the quest which you are undertaking this summer. Annie Amerika, you truly are turning a dream into a reality. Carol is John's ex-wife and the mother of his eldest child, Eric. Carol and her husband, Pat, have been good friends of ours for many years. Pat passed away just three months after John. Eric lost his father and stepfather, two important people in his life, within three months of each other.

Bonnie: My heart travels with you on your journey.

You're doing an incredible job with what life has handed you. Great lemonade Girl! Hugs.

Angie: Damn, Girl....have a great time and be safe! Love you!

Patty: Dear Anne Amerika

Your patriotism is astonishing and has made me even more proud to be an American. For you, I have 175 flags that are on 24 inch sticks, the flags measure 8 inch x 9 inch. They are great to hand out to people, place on grave sites or fly on bikes. I would like to donate them too you.

May 1, 2012

Thank you, Kimberly at Signs Etcetera.

Stars and stripes forever.
Each star has the name of a sponsor on it.

May 3, 2012

37 days and counting...

Hand held flags arrived today, thanks to the donation from Patty. They are much bigger than I thought they would be and oh, what joy I will have in giving these away! Hopefully one day our paths will cross and we can meet.

I gave most of these flags to children I met along the way. I also gave some to the children at Bridgeport Elementary School before I left.

Comments

Patty: I am so glad that these flags have gone to a good cause. I can't think of a better way to see them distributed - In Honor of a Vietnam Veteran by a Loving Wife. Thank You Annie Amerika!

More super stars:

Carol
Springer Tech

Brewster, Washington

May 11, 2012

Thank you, American Legion Post No. 108, Manson, Washington, for supporting me and my efforts in my journey to spread patriotism this summer. You say the memories I "will gain from this endeavor will be ever-lasting." So very true. Thank you!

May 12, 2012

I went camping this weekend with my friend Teresa, one last campout before I left on my journey. While there I met Boy Scout Troop 490 from Newman Lake, Washington. I donated a tattered flag for them to retire. Thank you, boys!

Comments

Juli: And it starts...

Luana: Oh yes the journey has begun!!

Boy Scout Troop 490 from Newman Lake, Washington

May 20, 2012

Chelan Sidecar Rally

I had so much fun meeting these patriotic men and women who rode hacks this weekend. I was even asked to be a monkey and join in on the games. Thank you for your support.

Two couples there belonged to a Christian Motorcycle Club and asked if they could bless my van before I leave. They came to me on Sunday morning and said a beautiful prayer for good luck on my trip. It was beautiful.

Comments

Der Biermann: Good meeting you @ CSR4. I was impressed by your story - it is an honorable pursuit. Best wishes!

May 21, 2012

Thank you VFW Post 3617 for your support! www.vfwpost3617.org. I was contacted by the VFW Post 3617 from Wenatchee, Washington, to see if I wanted a donation of new American flags. I told them I did need some of the large 4x6 flags. The VFW Post 3617 donated many large 4x6 flags.

John's memorial marker at Tahoma National Veterans Cemetery in Kent, Washington.

May 26, 2012

Today I went to the Bridgeport Cemetery to help set up flags for Memorial Day weekend. Many local students from Bridgeport Elementary School showed up to help. As we were putting up hundreds of flags, I couldn't help but wonder if a student in Kent, Washington, was putting up a flag on John's memorial marker at the Tahoma National Cemetery. Thank you, whoever you are, thank you.

May 28, 2012

I received an e-mail from a man named John; he wanted to know why I chose to spell America with a "k" as in Annie Amerika. First, I want everyone to know that in no way did I choose to spell it this way to be disrespectful or to make a political statement.

Before I set up my blog, email and Facebook page, I searched to see if anyone had used the name Annie America. Annie America was indeed taken, so I sent her an e-mail asking if she would give up the name so I could use it for my journey. I waited a few weeks and didn't hear anything.

It was at that time that I looked for other names to use, but I really wanted Annie America. So I decided to change the spelling of America to Amerika so I could secure the media forms I chose, those being my Gmail account, Facebook page and this blog. I am extremely sorry if I offended our country, it was not my intent. I love our country!

Comments

Patty: Annie Amerika,
I stand behind you 100%, This shows your dedication to include the good ole USA one way or another. I respect the fact that you made AMERIKA your own and AMERICA still belongs to everyone. I think it is all about perspective and it is impossible to make every person happy. PLEASE continue your journey knowing you are spreading patriotism far & wide.

Victoria: Didn't offend anyone here! I think it cute . . . . keep up the great work!

Maureen: It's a legitimate question, I'm glad you answered it...

Jody: Anyone lucky to know you knows you wouldn't do anything to offend-only to honor your husband

Claudia: An appropriate question that seemed to be asked without malice. It never occurred to me to ask you. He was curious and thanks to him, your answer told the story. Thanks.

June 2, 2012

Today would have been our wedding anniversary. I couldn't think of a better way to spend the day than telling everyone about John's love for his country.

I attended Bridgeport Daze in my hometown and met some wonderful people. I told many people about my journey and handed out small handheld American flags to the children in my community. I received enough donations to purchase five new flags. Thank you for supporting my travels in my quest to spread patriotism.

June 4, 2012

Thank you, Nancine, for your love and support! Nell's Café in Bridgeport rocks!

Nancine donated for the purchase of new American flags and enough quarters for laundry to last the entire trip. Nancine also contacted me many times during my trip to see if I needed anything. Thank you for your support, Nancine.

June 6, 2012

To me, patriotism is the love I have for my country as I support those who serve and defend it.

My patriotism also inspires me to change for the betterment of mankind as I deeply care for our country's citizens.

Comments

Nancine: Annie, you are a true patriot. I am proud and honored to call you my friend

Nancine told me that during the Vietnam conflict, she and a friend hand-stitched American flags and sent them to the troops in Vietnam. What an amazing thing to do.

June 8, 2012

Many people may want to know how I could take the entire summer off for this trip. Well, I work as a Para-Educator for Bridgeport School District and have summers off. What a perfect opportunity!

Comments

Claudia: Steve and I are so excited to follow along on you journey which is to start very soon. Good luck and God Bless you and America!

3

TIME TO SPREAD PATRIOTISM

June 9, 2012

Today is the day!

I intended on leaving Sunday, June 10, but when I got off work yesterday I realized that I can't wait another day. I am so excited!

So today is my first day of spreading patriotism, John's way: spontaneous, freely and organically. It is normally difficult for me to be spontaneous, but in John's true spirit I am leaving today, because this trip is about him.

Leaving Bridgeport, Washington, with 112,039.5 miles on my odometer. It is 58 degrees right now and cloudy. Sunrise today was 4:59 a.m.

Comments

Eric: Safe travels!

Sara: Don't forget the sunglasses!

Jody: I knew you'd leave early! Have an amazing journey. I pray you got good news at 3:00 yesterday and you are safe and happy!

Debra: Have fun, stay safe.

Der Biermann: Good weather for starting out, too. Safe trip!

Taegen: carpe diem! safe travels!

Bambi: Have a great time, and stay safe!!!

Luana: You are an amazing person Annie, here's to patriotism and meeting wonderful people...stay safe on your journey!!

Maureen: Have a blast and be safe

Shirley: Travel safely and enjoy every minute of your adventure! You are awesome!

Sara: Enjoy - what a wonderful trip it will be!!!!

Carol: May your trip be filled with memories whether it best reliving old memories or creating new ones. Many of us will be following you as you embark on this most special journey. Love and safe travels.

Loretta: Safe journeys!! There are a lot of people praying for you!

Barbara: We are so excited and honored to have you here!! See you tomorrow!!

Nancine: You go girl! I will be praying for you!!! God Bless the USA!!!

112,039.5 miles on the odometer.

May 2012

Dave and Suzy of Bridgeport, Washington, were the recipients of the first free flag.

I had driven up and down the roads in Bridgeport for a few weeks looking for the first flag to be replaced and found a few tattered flags flying in my community. When the time finally came for me to give away a flag, most people had already replaced their tattered flags. I approached Suzy and Dave to see if they wanted to be the first recipients. We talked about the size of their flagpole and thought they needed a bigger flag than they already had. I special ordered this flag just for them.

You're probably wondering why this post is dated in May. When I found the home of Dave and Suzy in Bridgeport, I told them what I was going to be doing this summer and wanted their flag to be the first replaced. They agreed and I ordered the beautiful 5' x 8' American flag. This was the only flag that I paid for out of my own pocket; the rest were donated. Once the flag came in, I couldn't wait until June 9 to give it to them so in early May, I presented them with their new American flag.

Comments

Maureen: Looks great.

Luana: Alright, go Annie Amerika!!

Carol: And so begins the quest.

Dave and Suzy hoisting up their new 5x8 American flag.
Bridgeport, Washington

June 10, 2012
First night.
I decided to leave early and head to one of my favorite campgrounds, Hawk Creek Campground. While there I met a nice couple from Spokane, Russ and Donna, and we talked. They wanted to support me on my trip so they brought over some of the best pork chops I have ever eaten and some potato salad, and they invited me for breakfast the next morning. Russ had told me that he had been camping at Hawk Creek for 45 years. What a wonderful hidden gem. Thanks, Russ and Donna.

First night on the road at Hawk Creek Campground.

Every afternoon when I stopped, I would put up my flag on my telescoping flagpole so everyone would know how proud I am to be an American.

First day on the road was a little rough. I cried. That evening I sat at my campsite in my chair looking out over the lake and cried softly at first, tears falling down my cheeks. I started crying harder as I thought about John and our special love, and his love for his country. Before I knew it, it was dark and I was still crying.

This is when I reminded myself that I shouldn't use the terms should have, could have or would have, because that is unknown territory and painful. I thought about how John would have loved this trip; after all, it was his idea. Then I reminded myself that thinking about what John would have, could have or should have done should not be my focus.

Comments

Joni: I envy you on this trip - you are going to meet some truly wonderful people. You attract them because you are one as well

Barbara: We are so excited to meet you!

Jennifer: Thanks for sharing your adventure with us! You're an amazing lady and John would be so proud of you.

Joe: It's going to be a great trip.

June 10, 2012

I stopped today and gave away a 3x5 American flag to Doug of Valley, Washington. He gave me the worn and tattered flag so I can give it to a scouting troop. What a great day!

It felt wonderful to give a perfect stranger, someone I never talked to before, a new American flag in memory of John. I stood by myself in front of his new flag and recited the Pledge of Allegiance and felt so proud to be an American.

Doug
Valley, Washington

Comments

Karen; What an honor to know you even if it's on fb. Thank you for what you're doing in honor of your husband. I Salute you!

Teresa: yeahhhhh.........the trip begins. Next it is to Barbara's house to raise a new flag and lower a tattered one and have the Boy Scouts perform a retirement ceremony.

June 10, 2012

Late this afternoon I was able to give Barbara and Hoss of Valley, Washington, a new American flag. Also at their home were 16 members of Boy Scout Troop 989 from Valley and Kellie Trudeau from *The Independent* newspaper. The boys put up the new flag and retired the old. It was the first time I attended the retirement ceremony of an American flag. Thank you everyone for helping me make John's dream come true, and thank you for being proud patriotic Americans.

Comments

Dorie: So very awesome :) And what a great experience for those boys...they made an amazing memory today :)

Carlen: We have a flag burning retirement ceremony at our annual AMA camping trip. The guy who does it reads what each fold represents and the history of the flag. It's very moving and every American should bare witness of such a patriotic event.

Pet Portraits By Cy: Thank you Annie, and safe Travels!

Tobi: What a wonderful experience for everyone involved! I can't wait to read more about your journey!

Boy Scout Troop 989 from Valley, Washington.

Barbara and Hoss
Valley, Washington

June 11, 2012

I only drove a short distance today, from Valley, Washington to Cheney, Washington. I drove up and down many streets looking to give a flag to a patriotic homeowner. Unfortunately for me, all the flags flying were in great condition. Good job, Cheney! Tomorrow I will look to give away two American flags.

While I was in Cheney I met with Othello Richards from KREM2 news. He followed me as I looked to give away a new American flag.

Comments
Marjorie: When you get to Enid, I know an address with a slightly tattered flag. We may only let you replace it if you stay 2 nights, though.

June 11, 2012
KREM 2 News did a nice story about my trip, see Chapter 5.

On June 12, 2012 I went to the home of our daughter, Sierra, and her husband, Brett, of Cheney, Washington. We shared a wonderful dinner and conversation. I spent the night sleeping in my van and left Cheney in the morning.

Sierra and Mom.

Sierra's prayer
"Lord, protect and guide my mom on her journey she is about to take. Watch over her and protect her from accidents. Keep her body and soul free from harm. Support her with your grace when she is tired and weak. Let her feel the presence of Dad, her angel, throughout the trip and mend and heal her soul as a result."

My television interview appeared that evening on KREM2 news out of Spokane. Later I went to the store and two women came up to me in the parking lot to say they saw me on television. They wished me luck on my trip, and the two women "kissed" my van for safe travels. That put a big smile on my face.

Comments

Diane: Great job keep it going. "We wish you all the best and hope you enjoy your trip" your friends Ralph and Diane from your Lake Chelan trip.

De: Annie, Saw your story on the news and wanted to say that I think what you are doing is wonderful. As a widow myself, I can say that this experience will probably facilitate your recovery from the huge loss of your husband, it a special way. He would be so proud of your for carrying out on of his dreams and making it yours too. I think you will be greatly blessed by what you are doing. DE.

Maureen: I am so proud of you Sister...

Lee Vonne: Dear Gayle, I just saw your story from the news - May God keep you safe on this journey!! Thank you for what you are doing - wish I could have gone with you!!

June 12, 2012

The long way to Clinton, Montana

What a wonderful day, so full of patriotic people. Today I left Cheney and headed through Newport, Washington, where I gave away a flag away to Hazel and Tom. When I went to the door Hazel said she saw me on the TV this morning and she told *me* my story; it made my heart sing.

After leaving Newport I drove east to Plain, Montana and talked to some nice folks at the VFW. Next, was the American Legion in Paradise, Montana (Hi Mo). While I was at the American Legion a man by the name of Robert from Hamilton, Montana came in, we talked a bit before I replaced some small flags at the park across the street from the American Legion.

I saw many American flags were flying everywhere. I am so proud to be an American! I'm spending the night at Rock Creek Lodge, Clinton, Montana (Hi Leo!). Tomorrow headed to West Yellowstone, Montana.

Hazel and Tom
Newport, Washington

June 13, 2012

Today I gave a flag to a proud Vietnam veteran by the name of Tom Hamilton. When I told Tom I didn't need a last name because I was trying to protect people's privacy and identity, he stated he had nothing to hide and was a proud veteran. The next page is Tom with his new American flag.

Tom Hamilton
Ennis, Montana

Robert was the proud recipient of today's second flag. Robert flies three flags - the American flag, the Marine flag, and POW/MIA flag. I was able to replace the American and POW/MIA flags for him. He told me he fought in WWII, Korea and Vietnam.

He was in the Marines for 31 years.

Robert had a kind of spunk in his voice, his smile and body that made you realizes he is a survivor. When I left Ennis, Montana, I was on a high from giving away flags, ecstatic and joyful to be meeting these men and finding out why they fly the American flag.

Veterans are the backbone to our country and we must never forget them.

Robert
Ennis, Montana

June 14, 2012

235 years ago today.

On June 14, 1777, the Continental Congress passed a resolution directing that "the flag of the thirteen United States be thirteen stripes, alternate red and white; that the union be thirteen stars, white in a blue field representing a new constellation."

The resolution marked the birthday of the flag known to us as the Stars and Stripes, which is why we observed Flag Day on June 14 of every year. Happy birthday to our flag and happy Flag Day!

I camped in West Yellowstone in a nice campground, but it was cold.

I huddled under blankets on my bed tonight, trying to stay warm.

There was a constant freezing rain coming down. Little did I know that this was good weather compared to what lie ahead.

June 14, 2012

Today I drove through Yellowstone National Park and I got to see Old Faithful erupt; beautiful!

Yellowstone National Park

Tatanka

After I saw Yellowstone National Park I drove to Cody, Wyoming. I was amazed at the "Spirit of America" on this magnificent Flag Day. American flags were everywhere. They were along the sides of the streets and most of the houses had beautiful, crisp flags flying.

I drove up and down for about an hour and couldn't find any that needed replacing, so I stopped into the local Veterans of Foreign Wars Post No. 2673 and talked to Russ, Glenn and Jim. They were not able to help me find any worn flags but mentioned they have been working hard at keeping new flags in the community. A woman there asked if I had seen their first annual Cody "Field of Honor." I hadn't, so I headed up the hill and it was inspirational, to say the least. It was hosted by the Cody Heritage Museum.

I then became more determined to find a flag to replace. I drove up and down streets for almost three hours and finally found Helen.

Helen didn't realize the flag was tattered because her husband took care of that type of stuff, he passed away in November 2011, one year after John died. I raised the flag and we recited the Pledge of Allegiance together. She had some more tattered flags and gave them to me.

Instantly I felt this bond with Helen, but most importantly, I could see and feel the pain she was suffering from her loss. When I realized I had a year more than her of healing, I wanted to help take her pain away and realized others are in just as much pain as I am, and possibly more.

I went to the visitor center and talked with Glen, who gave me the name and number for Bruce, executive director and chief executive officer for the Buffalo Bill Historical Center. I talked with him and I will bring the tattered flags to him tomorrow morning; he will give them to the Buffalo Bill Boy Scout Camp.

Helen
Cody, Wyoming

Cody, Wyoming has to be one of the most patriotic cities I have ever visited, or could it be that it was Flag Day? No, I do believe that they are the most patriotic city in America!

I slept in my first Wal-Mart parking lot and met a wonderful couple from Redding, California. Bill was smoking a cigar. I love the smell of his cigars, and it reminds me of my father!

Comments

Bill and Carolyn: Annie, proud of what you are doing. We were the ones in the Jamboree Motorhome parked in front of you in the Cody Wal-Mart. I was smoking a cigar and you said you like the smell. Keep up the good work.

First Annual Field of Honor in Cody, Wyoming.

I left Cody, Wyoming on the morning of June 15, 2012 and stopped by my childhood friend Joni's dad house, unexpected. It was wonderful meeting him. Richard was in the Navy in a program called "Kiddie Cruiser" where you enlist under the age 18 and are discharged before age 21.

Richard and myself.
Cody, Wyoming

June 15, 2012

The Good, the Bad and the UGLY

The good: My van overheated about five miles west of Cody near M&P Repair (thank you Jerry and Jodi).

The bad: The radiator cap was in bad shape. After replacing it I left and it overheated again, so back to M&P.

The ugly: After pressure washing the radiator it was determined I needed a new fan clutch and possibly a thermostat. Both were replaced and I feel very lucky to have Jerry and Jodi in my life right now, and Lucy the dog. I will keep everyone posted.

Comments

Butch: Sorry for the problems, hope the rest of the trip is all good.

Carol: Glad you found a shop that you can trust.
Hopefully you will quickly be back on the road.
Kaye: Sorry to hear about your car trouble, but
wanted you to know what a fantastic adventure
you're on, keep up the good work
Annie Amerika 2012: water pump is shot also...
another adventure in the life of me.
Marjorie: Oh no! Praying for you!
Edog: Well you did not expect this to be easy did
you? Give us a call if we can help with anything. Eric
Annie Amerika 2012: Hi Eric, I did not expect this to
be an easy trip, and I was prepared for little bumps
in the road. But when it actually happened I couldn't
help but to think how I wish your dad was here with
me now. I am a strong woman and a survivor, but I
sure do miss him!
  Today I did not replace any worn flags, but what an
adventurous day it was. My van overheated just five
miles west of Cody, Wyoming. Since I drive a 1985
Chevy van I was prepared for some distractions along
the way, and this was one of those distractions.
I did anticipate minor breakdowns, but as anyone
who has lost a spouse knows, anything that happens
in a negative way feels escalated. I remember when I
had to move a few months after John died and I
couldn't hook up the VCR/DVD player to the
television. I sat on the floor in the fetal position and
cried hysterically. If he hadn't died, I wouldn't have
to try to figure this out. I went online and reread the
booklet, but couldn't figure it out. After four hours of
crying and trying, I finally called Eric, my step-son,
whom I love as a son. He helped me in a matter of
minutes in his calm, reassuring voice.
This breakdown was the same thing; instantly I was
almost hysterical. When I realized I broke down in
front of a mechanic shop and someone was coming
out to help me, I realized I had broken down in the
perfect place. Was John watching over me?
  I was still worried about the cost I might endure. I
brought the title with me on this trip just in case I
didn't have the funds to fix the van; I could sign over

the title and take the Greyhound bus home. I'm so glad that didn't happen.

Jerry, my mechanic, dropped what he was doing and spent the day working on my van. He started with the radiator cap, which I had known might be in need of replacement. When that didn't help he pressured washed the bugs out of my radiator, then he realized my fan clutch wasn't working properly. That led us to the water pump and the thermostat. Jerry ran into a few other problems, but fixed them with his creative mind.

While Jerry was working on my van, I sat inside with Jodi. Jodi is the office person, receptionist, and parts runner, and she is dating Jerry. I explained my story to Jodi and she made sure I had what I needed for a low price. I found that Jodi is a biker and that they were getting ready for a benefit run for a friend who was having medical difficulties. I donated a gift card for the auction. I was so appreciative of their many hours of hard work that I gifted them with a new American flag.

Jodi and Jerry
Cody, Wyoming

I traveled from Cody toward Sheridan over the most beautiful scenic road I have ever been on. It was also the first time in my life I drove above the 9,000-foot elevation. I did not make it tonight to my intended destination of Sturgis, South Dakota, but I did get to shower at the Flying J in Gillette, Wyoming - my first shower since I left my daughter's home in Cheney, Washington - and will have a peaceful night sleep. I'm ready for a new day to spread patriotism one flag at a time.

When I woke up the next morning, I headed toward Spearfish, South Dakota. I took a short cut between Greybull and Sheridan, Wyoming. The Bighorn Scenic Byway (US 14) connects these cities and has 45 miles of Scenic Mountain driving. Do you know the area I'm talking about? Let's just say I'm so glad my mechanical problems were fixed in Cody.

The Big Horn Mountains are amazing. They have markers on the different type of rock formations that tell you what type of rock it is and approximately how old it is. I took this photo at the top of Granite Pass.

June 16, 2012

It's about the people you meet in life. This morning I headed to White's Queen City Motors (Chevy dealer) in Spearfish, South Dakota. My van ran rough all day yesterday and I thought it would be a great idea to have it checked out. Ethan was my mechanic, Jake is service advisor and then there was Kree. Kree should be "Employee of the Year." They got me in right away. Ethan found a cracked spark plug wire, replaced it and they got me out in a very short time. A special thank you to Kree. Good things happen to good people. Yours is coming!

On a side note, Kree paid for my repair out of her own pocket after hearing my story. How truly blessed I am. Thank you again, Kree!

Comments

Cathy: Ahhhhhhhh, praying for your protection and provision and God's perfect peace today.

June 16, 2012

I spent the night in Spearfish, South Dakota, and when I left I stopped in Sturgis, South Dakota and replaced the flag of Harvey and Edna. They have been married over 60 years and Harvey tells me he was in World War I; he enlisted when he was 17 years old. Hats off to Harvey and Edna!

Harvey and Edna
Sturgis, South Dakota

I spent the afternoon walking around Sturgis. This is one of the stops where John and I had planned on spending some time. I enjoyed seeing the sights and stopping in a few establishments.

June 12, 2012
Sturgis RV Park is only two blocks from downtown, many things to see and do. But did you know that Sturgis RV Park has many wonderful people staying here? I met

Charlie from Vermont, and the nice lady from Florida, and the couple up on the hill.

Comments

Hi Annie, this is harleychick51. I am so glad I met you at Sturgis RV Park. You are one courageous woman to go it alone. Be careful and safe out there and my God bless.

I talked with a man named Charlie for quite some time; he gave me a pin and recommended the YouTube video "Reveille," which I posted at a later date. I proudly wear this pin on my jacket.

I received a message from my friend Aubrey, who is stationed at Ellsworth Air Force Base. I agreed to meet her in the morning.

June 16, 2012

So far I have spread patriotism 1,393.9 miles, throughout five states!

Comments

Angela: Praying for travel mercies for you.
Teresa: you rock
Jasper: This is so awesome. Thank you Annie
Aubrey: Simply amazing

June 17, 2012

Father's Day

John was the father of three amazing children, and it is in John's honor that I give away American flags.

John's three amazing children

This morning I met up with Aubrey. We hadn't seen each other in a few years and she has grown into a magnificent woman. I am proud to call her my friend, but I am honored that she is serving our country!

After meeting with Aubrey I headed to Mount Rushmore National Memorial, a place John and I had talked about visiting. While I was there I noticed some military personal and briefly told them my story and thanked them for their service. Here is a photo of me with a couple of our nation's heroes.

June 17, 2012

After I left Mt. Rushmore National Memorial, I decided to head west on Highway 44; it turned out to be a lonely road. I stopped in Winner, South Dakota, drove up and down the streets for a while when I found a flag in need of retirement, and I presented Francis with a new American flag.

She invited me into her home; normally I would graciously decline, but today was hot. Francis told me it was 102 degrees. So I went into her air-conditioned home. She told me about the nine children she had, and shared her life stories with me. It was nice to get to know her, and cool off at the same time. I bid her a farewell and headed to the Missouri River.

Comments

Teresa: Dang girl talk about changing the way you see the world on a very deep and personal level.
Pat: another entry in you travel journal, so wonderful memories, and the lives you have touched, great job girl.

After leaving the home of Francis, I couldn't help but wonder if her family would be upset with her for letting a stranger into her home. It was then that I realized how many people are lonely and in need of someone to talk to.

I vowed to spend time with shut-ins. When I got home I contacted my friend who is affiliated with the local church, and she is working on setting me up with someone I can be a companion to.

Francis
Winner, South Dakota

Yes, Francis, it was a hot day.

June 18, 2012

Today is a day of healing.

I spent the night at Buryanek State Recreational area in South Dakota, then continued east on highway 44 until I got to Sioux Falls. I headed north on 29 until I reached Flandreau. I realized I was going pretty far out of my way and headed back south on 75 through Pipestone and on into Luverne, Minnesota. I headed east on Interstate 90 and am camped the night at a Wal-Mart parking lot.

**** So where does the healing take place? ****

Here I am in a place I didn't intend to be, and out of nowhere I see a Minnesota Veterans Home. I turned my van around and pulled in because I felt the need to volunteer my time. I was met by their gracious employees and met Duane, the volunteer services coordinator. I told him my story and I asked if I could visit with some of the residents. The first person he set me up with was their eldest resident, a woman. I let her talk, and I listened. She was a feisty woman and we got along well.

Duane then took me to meet a man who was in the Korean War. This man helps with the recycling and actually crushes the cans with his hands by twisting the can and then compressing it. He immediately told me the story of a Korean woman he befriended and her daughter. He said that she helped him many times by hiding him behind a curtain under the sink because he knew he didn't belong there. He said all the women in that town were killed, including the woman he befriended, but always wondered what happened to the girl. He talked, I listened. He asked

49

me to find her. I asked him what her name was and he didn't know. I asked where she lived and he didn't know the name of the town. With urgency in his voice, he asked me to find her. I felt so bad for his pain, pain he had been holding for over 60 years. This is when I realized just how blessed I have been. Today was a day of healing.

When I left, Duane sent me off with a bag of gifts, including my new favorite coffee cup. They were such nice people.

Listening is a healing tool for me because when I hear the pain in someone else's story, it makes me realize my pain isn't that bad. This man has hung onto the hope of finding a little girl for 60 years! He is sharing his story and pain with me, a perfect stranger. I couldn't imagine holding pain for 60 years. This was the beginning of the healing process for me, listening.

Things happen for a reason in life and it was no mistake going to Flandreau, because if I hadn't turned back down and headed through Luverne, the magic wouldn't have happened.

Minnesota Veterans Home
Luverne, Minnesota

Before I went to the Minnesota Veterans Home, I stopped in Parkston, South Dakota, where I met Donald and Vernetta. Donald is a Korean vet, and he appreciated the new flag. My next stop was just down the street, where I found Lawrence and Alice.

Lawrence was a little apprehensive, but accepted the new flag. I asked if he was in the military and he said, "A long time ago." He was a man of few words, and from his tone he didn't want to talk about it.

Donald and Vernetta
Parkston, South Dakota

Lawrence and Alice
Parkston, South Dakota

Comments

Teresa: I hope you sleep well tonight my friend. What you are doing is a blessed adventure; you are bringing joy, pride and recognition to a lot of wonderful patriots. In fact I would say they needed you. Needed you to remind them that they are what makes America a great land, the Land of the Free, the home of the Brave. Yup I would say they needed you to remind them they are appreciated and necessary in these difficult times for our country. Thank you

June 19, 2012

Good morning Worthington, Minnesota. Sunrise today is 5:40 a.m., the current temperature is 73 degrees, today I have logged a total of 2,000 miles!

June 19, 2012

I love Iowa!

This morning I left Worthington, Minnesota and headed east on I-90 to Austin, home of the Spam Museum. I love Spam, and now they have it in garlic and jalapeno! Which shall I have for dinner?

When I was done at the museum, I drove around and found Harlan, a Korean-era veteran. He said he usually changes out his flag on the Fourth of July, but he accepted the new flag from me. It was a big one at 4x6, but I had a few on hand just in case. After we got the new flag up I was able to meet his beautiful wife, June.

Harlan and June
Austin, Minnesota

After I left Harlan and June's house, I headed south east toward Cresco, Iowa, where I drove up and down the streets until I met Roger. Roger stated he was in the Army during the Vietnam conflict. After gifting him with a new flag I went to the visitor center, the post office, the local newspaper and the farmers market. They have a beautiful community.

Roger
Cresco, Iowa

While at the farmers market, I bought a few things form Cardinal Acres Produce. Their motto is "fresh-all natural-locally grown," just the way I like it. I fell in love with this town! When someone says "America's Heartland," they must have visited Cresco, Iowa.

June 20, 2012

Argyle, Wisconsin

I slept very well last night, considering the raccoons woke me up twice. You see, I had left my basil plant outside and they "played in the dirt." They didn't eat the basil, though. I headed east on Highway 18 and before I knew it I was at Cave of the Mounds State Park. I didn't plan it that way; you see I missed my turn off headed south. While there I met a young dad and his two small children. They liked my van. I gave the children each a small hand held American flag. It made me smile.

I headed south and found myself in Argyle, Wisconsin. Have you been here? If you had, you would remember this town and its people. I had been driving up and down the streets for about 45 minutes when I found Audrey; she was taking care of her grandchildren, and they desperately needed a flag. The home was just adorable!

We talked some and I gave the two children each a hand held American flag and raised the new 3x5 American flag. They said the Pledge of Allegiance with me, and I took a photo of the children in front of the new flag.

What I want you to know about Audrey is that her handshake was strong, she looked me in the eye and thanked me, and it was a special moment. Thank *you*, Audrey. When I got ready to leave, she recommended I stop at the *Pecatonica Valley Leader*, the local paper, and talk to Gary. I stopped and explained my circumstance to Gary as he wrote as fast as he could. He took some photos; hopefully I'll be in their newspaper next week showing how I spread patriotism, one flag at a time. And tonight, I will get to do some fishing!

Audrey
Argyle, Wisconsin

After I gave the new flag to Grandma Audrey, I received some private messages from Maureen, the mother of the littlest one in the photo. This is the home of Maureen and her family. For privacy reasons I'm not going to publish all her comments, but will post some excerpts from them:

"Hello, I am Maureen, from Argyle, WI. I was wondering if you would like a copy of the article that was in our local newspaper, it was very nice article and nice pictures too. I thank you very much for the flag. My daughter is so proud of it and of the small one you gave her; she put it in her flowers that night. I truly do appreciate you giving us a new one, wish I could have met you myself. So, if you would like a copy of the newspaper I would be more than willing to send you a

copy but need your address. Thank you again for stopping by Argyle, WI; it is a wonderful little town. Best of luck on your travels and have a safe trip back home. God Bless You!
"Maureen"

June 21, 2012

The summer solstice started last night; that means today is the first full day of summer!

Sunrise in Lena, Illinois was 5:17 a.m. this morning.

I have been on the road for 11 full days, traveling 2,431.3 miles through nine states and I have given away 18 flags.

Today I will visit my daddy in Antioch, Illinois!

Comments

Joni: Give your dad a (((hug))) for me!

Diane: Hope you have a great visit with your Dad

Maureen: Give him a hug for me too!

Der Biermann: Awesome!

Lena, Illinois Veterans Memorial.

June 21, 2012

Today I traveled from Lena, Illinois back up through Wisconsin and down Highway 83 into Antioch, Illinois to my father's house. After we visited for a while, I showered and headed out to give away another American flag. I found a tattered flag at Jill's home. She told me her family has lived in Antioch for many generations. She recited the pledge of alliance with me and I left two hand held flags for her children.

Jill told me that she was home from work today because she had her wisdom teeth pulled. She seemed to be in pain, but I was glad she let me put up a new flag for her.

Comments

Jill: It was lovely meeting you! Thanks again for stopping! What a wonderful thing you are doing.

Jill
Antioch, Illinois

My first night at my father's house, we had a party that included my sister Elizabeth; her son Jesse, his wife Katie and their children; JR and Jayden, also there was my other nephew, Joshua and my niece Lisa and her husband, Rob. We had a wonderful family dinner and I enjoyed the conversations. Later I went online and contacted the local Boy Scout troop. They will meet me in two days to receive tattered flags for retirement.

June 22, 2012

I want to thank my nephew Jesse for changing the oil in my van and getting me ready for my next leg of the journey and for purchasing a Chilton motor manual, just in case.

Dakota, Elizabeth, Jesse, Jayden, Josh, Annie, Katie, Lisa and Rob.

June 23, 2012

Today has been a very busy one. The first thing I did was meet up with Boy Scout Troop 190 at the Antioch Veterans of Foreign Wars Post No. 4551 to deliver tattered flags. It was John's hope that all Scouts would learn proper flag retirement etiquette.

Scout master Tom was there to accept the flags, and the boys took a few minutes to properly fold them. I talked about my mission of replacing worn and tattered American flags to unsuspecting homeowners. While we talked Tom, VFW Commander for Post No. 4551, arrived. We enjoyed some conversation, took some photos and I was off to find yet another unsuspecting homeowner.

Tom told me about a welcome home party tomorrow at Lake Villa VFW to welcome home Michael Anthony Soto. I did a little research and found that the Patriot Guard will be riding along with the motorcade. John was a Patriot Guard Rider.

Comments

Betty: you're looking younger. I think this trip agrees with you.

Lynette: I agree. I think this mission in life is healing your heart, Gale. Keep on truckin girl!! Luv you!

Annie Amerika 2012: it is doing my soul good.

Frank: Annie is in Antioch, IL!! She visited with Boy Scout Troop 190, handed over some retired flags. Everyone had a great time.

Antioch, Illinois Boy Scout Troop No. 190.

June 23, 2012

Today's flag went to Laura of Lake Villa, Illinois!

Laura was apprehensive and stayed inside her home, looking out the front door.

Laura
Lake Villa, Illinois

Today I also stopped to get my van washed by the Antioch High School field hockey team. I graduated from Antioch High School and wanted to support my school. I never made it back to any of my high school reunions, so this was a special moment for me.

Thank you, girls!

Antioch High School field hockey team.

June 23, 2012

I will be at the VFW in Lake Villa, Illinois tomorrow at 2:30 p.m. to talk about my travels. Hope to see you there.

June 24, 2012

I pledge allegiance to the flag of the United States of America and to the Republic for which it stands, one Nation under God, indivisible, with liberty and justice for all.

We recite the Pledge of Allegiance as a promise of loyalty to the United States. The Pledge of Allegiance was first published in September 1892 in a magazine called the Youth's Companion. The magazine printed it to help celebrate the 400th anniversary of Columbus reaching America.

The original words read: "I pledge allegiance to my Flag and to the Republic for which it stands, one Nation indivisible, with liberty and justice for all." In the early 1920s it was changed from "my flag" to "the flag of the United States of America." Congress added the phrase "under God" in 1954.

June 24, 2012

Today I will be attending a homecoming for HM3 Michael Anthony Soto (Navy). He is coming home today from Afghanistan. The homecoming will be held at the Lake Villa VFW Memorial Post 4308. I'm looking forward to meeting him! Welcome home, Michael.

Comments
Luana: That's so exciting!!
Jennifer: Yes welcome home!!!!
Maureen: thank you Michael Anthony Soto!

June 24, 2012

Today I had a cathartic experience. This emotionally, spiritually and overwhelming experience was about a young man named Michael Anthony Soto, a name I will never forget. I didn't know about Michael until yesterday, when I heard he was coming home from Afghanistan. His family and friends held a welcome home party in Lake Villa, Illinois, at the VFW Memorial Post No. 4308.

Michael had a hero's welcome as he was led by officers of the law, Iron Justice MC and WWR (Warriors' Watch Riders). With the approval of Richard, All-State Team 2011-2012 Post Commander of this VFW and Michael's family, I presented Michael with a 4x6 Annin American flag on behalf of myself and my husband, John.

I did not give away an American flag to an unsuspecting homeowner today, but I feel that this flag was given to the right person today. Welcome home, HM3 Michael Anthony Soto, and thank you for your service!

Comments
Barbara: What an amazing experience! You seem to always be at the right place at the right time
Maureen: No such thing as a coincidence... you are exactly where you're supposed to be. Mom and John would be so proud of you.
Sandy: I did not officially meet you . . . when you were at the VFW in Lake Villa, IL...but from afar...you were and remain an inspiration to me. Safe travels always! Sandy F. (Volo, IL)

Presenting Michael with a new American flag.

June 25, 2012

I have spent three full days here in the Antioch/Lake Villa, Illinois area, but it is time to continue my journey. I still have 61 more flags to give away!

When I made it to the Cook County line in Illinois, I stopped for gas and saw a Blues Mobile. John loved the movie "The Blues Brothers," so I took a photo. It was tradition in our family to watch this movie on New Year's Eve. Unfortunately when I left the gas station, I was still looking at the Blues Mobile and went through a red light. I have been waiting for a ticket in the mail, but haven't received one yet.

It was a fun challenge trying to travel south from Antioch, Illinois through the Chicago area without going onto the toll roads and interstate. I made it to Morton Grove before I had to get on the interstate, but I did avoid all toll roads. After getting through Chicago I headed east into Indiana and up north into Michigan. I traveled east on Highway 12 until I stopped at a cute town called White Pigeon, Michigan. This is where I found the home of Pat and her husband, who were in need of a new American flag.

While I was putting up Pat's new flag, she told me she lost a brother in Vietnam as he was refueling a jet. She also told me her husband was a Korean War veteran, and she had a cousin that was a POW for six years. For these reasons they fly their American flag every day with pride. When we were done talking I felt like I had a new friend; she said the Pledge of Allegiance with me and gave me a hug. Off I went with the sun behind me.

Comments

Cathy: that is wonderful news. I bless each of you and honor the memories of the ones who served. My brother is a Vietnam vet. He is a hero too.

Annie Amerika 2012: Thank you Cathy, and please give your brother my sincere thanks for his service.

Chicago, Illinois

Pat
White Pigeon, Michigan

June 26, 2012

Good morning, America!

It's a beautiful day in Sturgis, Michigan. At 7:25 a.m. it's 52 degrees and sunny. I love a Wal-Mart parking lot that has accommodations for non-motorized vehicles.

I enjoyed listening to the conversations of the Amish visitors to Wal-Mart. The adults talked in a quiet voice with their tones never changing, but the children were just like children around the country. I could hear things like, "She's on my side" and "He touched me." I sat in my van laughing at the normalcy of children everywhere.

Sturgis, Michigan

June 26, 2012

Interesting information you may want to know:

- I only give flags to residences. I do not give flags to commercial businesses.
- The flags I have are for poles 12 to 25 feet tall; I do not have flags for home mount sticks.
- As I come into a town I look for old growth trees; these areas seem to have more flag poles.
- To find a home in need of a flag, I normally wait until early afternoon before I drive up and down streets. Most people are not home during the day.

• I have left about 20 calling cards to homeowners who were not home.

Yes, the flags are free.

Comments

Annie Amerika 2012: One more thing, this trip is NOT a political statement. I give away flags because it is our patriotic pride in this beautiful country.

Barb: hi, you left a card in my door, I live in Rome city, how to I get a new flag, mine is tattered and old, ty. (I sent Barb a private message.)

Kyona: You are amazing!!

Jenny: So proud of you!

June 26, 2012

Today I traveled south on Highway 9 until I met up with Cornfield Road, otherwise known as Highway 6. Today's flag went to Jose of Weston, Ohio. Jose told me he has a son currently serving in Iraq. Jose said he is very proud of his son.

Jose and his young son, Tyler, recited the Pledge of Allegiance with me, and Tyler posed with his hand over his heart for this photo.

Tonight I am staying at East Harbor State Park on Lake Erie, Ohio. Tomorrow I head to Avon Lake, Ohio.

I made the 3,000-mile mark today.

Jose's son, Tyler
Weston, Ohio

June 27, 2012

Today was adventurous all day long. It started with finding Diana of Port Clinton, Ohio. Her flag was badly tattered and she needed a new one. I asked her why she flew the flag and she said her parents always flew a flag; it was tradition. Thank you, Diana, for accepting the new American flag.

Diana
Port Clinton, Ohio

When I left Diana's home I headed to the local Wal-Mart to see if they did front end alignment; the front end of my van had been feeling a little squirrely. I quickly found they did not. Next, I headed to a car wash, and while washing my tires I noticed a chunk of the tire missing. I headed back to the Wal-Mart for new tires.

Did you know that they can't match existing tires if they are not to manufacturer recommendations? Me neither, so today I got four new tires.

From there I headed to the home of my co-worker's parents, and fell in love with Avon Lake, Ohio! Ed, Celeste and their son, Eric, treated me like family. After a wonderful dinner that Eric cooked for us, we headed to Lake Erie. Ed made a few stops and we ended up in Lorain on the dock by a magnificent light house.

There were many people fishing on the dock, and the sunset was stunning.

Thank you, Ed and Celeste, for your hospitability, and thank you Caitlin of Bridgeport, Washington, for having such wonderful parents. Tomorrow I will be talking at Ed's Lions Club.

June 28, 2012

Lube Stop Inc., you rock my world! My van has been running rough (once it warms up) since Cody, Wyoming, so I talked with Ed yesterday about my van and he thought it might be my PCV valve.

Today I went to The Lube Stop, Inc. in Avon Lake (Ed's recommendation), and they found the hose connecting to the PCV was off, they put it back on, topped my fluids, checked my tire pressure and charged me $0.00. If you have a Lube Stop in your area please visit them, they are knowledgeable, fast and friendly.

Thank you Jordan, Randy and especially Matt! I went onto Yelp and wrote a nice recommendation about this Lube Stop.

Comments

Jenny: Kind acts beget kind acts Annie America!
Annie Amerika 2012: After I left I went to the store and brought back some Gatorade and candy bars for them.

June 28, 2012

I don't even know where to start today. Blessed is the first thing that comes to mind. I spent a wonderful evening with Ed and Celeste in Avon Lake, Ohio (Norman Rockwell would be proud to call this town his own).

At noon I attended a Loraine Lions Club meeting. I was one of two speakers for the day. www.lorainlionsroar.blogspot.com. Steve Hall from Inglewood, Australia went first, talking about his mission for the Lions Club.

Next was my turn; I did well for the better part of my speech, but become emotional talking about John. After I was done, a few of the men came up and suggested I go to *The Morning Journal* to tell my story. By the time I got there, someone had already called in my story. I was interviewed by Jason Henry, and the story will run tomorrow, see story in Chapter 5. After I left *The Morning Journal* I headed to Geneva, Ohio. John grew up in Geneva, Ohio

He lived in Geneva until his family moved to Huntington Beach, California when he was 13 years old. I stopped in at Geneva Eagles No. 2243, "The Friendly Aerie," and I instantly felt comfortable.

Comments

Caitlin: Sounds like you had a great time, Gail! Good luck on the rest of your journey!

Pat: Make sure they all send you a copy of the paper for your remembrance album. Glad you're doing such a great job.

Steven: A truly humbling experience to find such a courageous Lady, carrying on the vision her Husband, John, had, Blessed.

Celeste: It is Annie aka Gail that is really the blessing. Getting to share her journey and story for just one evening was definitely inspirational!!

Thursday, June 28, 2012

Guest speakers from Washington and Australia
Lion Steve Hall (left) from Inglewood, Queensland, Australia and Gale Wilkison (right) from Bridgeport, Washington both spoke to Lorain Lions at our Thursday, June 28 noon meeting. Lion Steve talked about Lions in Australia, and Gale spoke about her project traveling the country this summer exchanging old American flags for brand new ones.

June 28, 2012

Last night I spent time with the good folks at Eagles in Geneva, Ohio. I slept in my van in their parking lot.

Fraternal Order of the Eagles No.2243 and me.

June 29, 2012

I did an interview with Jason Henry from *The Morning Journal* yesterday. He emailed me to say I will be on the front page Monday.

Comments

Claudia: This is so cool and will bring even further awareness!! Yay

Carol: Fantastic

Angie: You should call NBC, ABC and CBS too! And FOX!!

June 29, 2012

I found that the train runs through Geneva ALL night long; glad I like trains. Good morning, Geneva! Sunrise today was at 5:51 a.m., the temperature is 73 degrees (but feels like 93), and I have driven 3,184.3 miles. Today I'm off to find the home John was raised in. Although John was born in Ashtabula, he came home to the family home on Tuttle Road in Geneva, where he lived with his family until he was 13 years old. It feels really good to be in his hometown.

John as a small child in Geneva, Ohio.

This morning I went to Tuttle Road. The area is now owned by Waste Management, but they still have two old houses standing on the property. I talked to Evan and he stated that the home I took photos of could have been

John's home. He also said that there was an old home on the site of the new office. We will probably never really know, but he did give me the name and number of a woman to call later this afternoon.

Now I know why John liked to live in rural America; that is where he was raised.

June 29, 2012
This is the home I took photos of and believe is the childhood home of John and his family. It matches up with an old photo with John in front of a door and a window to his left.

John's childhood home.

I stopped at the home of Howard; his flag was worn and tattered. I told him my story and he said he was just thinking about replacing his flag this morning. The rope holding his flag crumbled as we took down the old flag, so he was off to the garage for new rope.

We chatted and I asked if he knew of John Wilkison; he asked if he had a sister named Gertrude! Yes, John's sister was Gertrude (Trudy). Howard was older than John and remembered him on the school bus with his sister Gertrude. Howard entered the Army in 1961 and was in

Korea. Today I gave a new American flag to someone who actually knew of John and his family!

When I was chatting with Howard, he told me he was a Chevy man and asked if I needed any work done on my van. I told him I did not (anymore). He asked me what I named her (my camper van), and I told him I didn't have a name. He said that he would name her Chevelitta, and we laughed. He also said to me, "Do you see that Jeep over there?" I said yes, and he said it had a perfectly good engine in it, but he took it out to put in a Chevy engine. Now that is a Chevy man.

I have since been in touch with Howard; he drove down Tuttle Road for me and confirmed that the house on the corner I took a photo of on Tuttle Road was the Wilkison house.

Howard
Geneva, Ohio

Comments

Cathy: That is really a sweet encounter. So happy for you.

Sara: Awesome!!!!

Lisa: You camped next to us at Geneva State park. It was wonderful meeting you--you brought tears to my eyes when you told us your plans. How wonderful that you found someone who knew John, and all by chance!

June 30, 2012

Yesterday I spent some time at the library in Geneva, Ohio, researching John's heritage, and realized I needed to head to Cleveland. John adored his grandfather and told me stories about their Sunday dinners at Shaker Square in Cleveland, Ohio. John said he would go up to the counter with his grandfather to pay the bill and his grandfather would always buy him butter rum Lifesavers.

Today I headed west into East Cleveland. Yes, I went backward a bit, but I went to Lake View Cemetery to see the burial place of my husband's grandfather.

First, I have to tell you that I have my navigation system set so it uses the shortest route and no highways. I traveled the back roads of East Cleveland and in areas that were quite repressed, and at times I felt uncomfortable.

Once at Lake View Cemetery I quickly found the grave marker for John E. Wilkison II and his wife, Gertrude Burrows Wilkison. There was also Mary Ellen Wilkison, the oldest of their three children. I took photos and said a little prayer, thanking them for bringing the Wilkison men into our lives. At the library yesterday I found the 1930 census, which said John and Gertrude Wilkison lived on Terrace Road in the Grandview area of East Cleveland. It also listed his occupation as a manufacturer of printing presses!

I recalculated my navigation and headed out, but soon I noticed almost an entire mile stretch of once lavish large homes, some four stories tall, but all seemed to be abandoned and in disrepair. Windows were broken, lawns overgrown; it was sad to think that someone lived there in luxury long ago. I decided at that time I did not want to find the home of John's grandfather, and to let it rest.

July 1, 2012

Good morning, America! It's July, my favorite month of the year!

Today I leave Ohio, the 12th state of my expedition.

Thirty-four flags have been distributed. My 1985 Chevy van and I have traveled 3,320.9 miles on this magnificent journey; today is my 22nd day on the road.

Comments

Maureen: Safe travels Annie

Jodi: Annie you are so awesome!! Happy trails to you

July 1, 2012

Prayers needed for a Marine Vietnam veteran by the name of Robert from Butler, Pennsylvania. I just gave a flag to his son, Jeremy, also a Marine. The pole had to be 30 feet tall and my 4x8 flag looks small upon it. Jeremy said they were getting ready to have a prayer vigil for his father, who has been battling cancer and had been for a couple years. So please take a moment out of your day and pray for Robert and his family, and pray for all those fighting courageously against this horrific disease.

Heavenly sunrise.

Jeremy
Butler, Pennsylvania

July 1, 2012

Today's journey took me into Pennsylvania. As you can see by my prior post, I gave a flag to Jeremy; he was in the Marines and so was his father, Robert. I'm honored to be able to give you a new flag. When I left Butler, I realized Pennsylvania had many rolling hills. Most of the day I felt like I was on a kiddie roller coaster, but it was fun. In the early afternoon I stopped at three Wal-Marts looking for a place to spend the night (all three didn't allow overnight camping/sleeping), so I headed to Kooser State Park.

I told the campground host that I was having a difficult time finding a Wal-Mart with overnight parking and he said that he knew of two that allowed it. I did not spend the night at Kooser State Park; instead I headed a bit out of my way to Wal-Mart. Tomorrow I think I'll stick with the main roads!

July 2, 2012
The newspaper article and video from *The Morning Journal*, Lorain, Ohio came out today, see Chapter 5.

Me and Charlie
Photo courtesy of Jason Henry

Charlie has been my constant companion on this journey. I started him by seed in January; I had hoped that I could eat fresh tomatoes this summer, but Charlie hasn't produced any flowers yet. Maybe my van is too hot?

July 2, 2012
Today is Monday, a day for many like any other Monday, but for me it was a unique day. This morning I went to the Flight 93 National Memorial. Who could forget what these patriotic people did on 9/11 to save us? "Let's roll."
The drive from the main road to the memorial was 3.5 miles, it was quiet and calm, almost eerily. Shortly after I arrived at the memorial I met Pam, a teacher from South Lyon, Michigan. We talked about that unforgettable day during our somber walk.
Fascinating information about Flight 93: It crashed going 563 mph, and although the crater was only 15 feet deep and 30 feet across, they found debris 45 feet below the surface. True heroes they are!
I left Flight 93 National Memorial and took the back roads headed toward Harpers Ferry, West Virginia. I should have reminded myself to take the main roads, but it was a glorious morning, so I traveled the back roads. I logged only 162.6 miles, but it took me eight hours. I crossed the Allegheny Mountains and the Potomac River, but please remind me to take the main roads next time!

Items left behind at Flight 93 National Memorial.

I found myself driving through Rohrersville, Maryland, and from the road I saw a tattered flag. I turned back and found the home of Mike; I gave him and new flag and asked him why he flies the American flag. With a proud strong tone in his voice, he said, "Because I'm a proud American."

Comments

Cathy: beautiful land......America. Bless Mike for being such a proud American.

Sandra: Yes, Maryland looks lovely

Sue: haha, Gale, you have asked to be reminded to stick to main roads before...I don't think you will! I think you secretly like the adventures you have on the back roads and smaller roads, where you really get to see America up close!!

Mike
Rohrersville, Maryland

July 2, 2012

This next photo is the road I accidently got on. I think they charge by how many feet you travel! It took 19 miles for the first exit and it did not have a return, just a few hours out of my way.

The next few days will be very hard on me emotionally. I want to thank everyone... family, friends and people I have met on the road ahead of time.

Comments

Joni: You know you have my support and love

Juli: I love you-we all love you.

Lise: The Wall is not an easy place to go at the best of times. I have been there and found it very emotional. Please, know you are in our thoughts and prayers on the 4th, and everyday along your entire journey.

Luana: We are all with you, take care!

Tobi: I so wish I could have been home to share this time with you. I find your courage and strength so inspiring, and am eternally grateful to have you as a role-model and friend. If you need any help with info about the area, don't hesitate to call or write. All my love...

Maureen: you're never more than a phone call away. Love you Seester

Cathy: prayers going out for you, Annie. God is able to keep you in the midst of the emotional storm. I know men whose names are on that wall. Holding you in my heart. Reading your posts and cheering you on in love.

Jenny: Let your emotions flow...and then remember how much you are making a difference!

July 3, 2012

Unsuspecting to Naomi of Harpers Ferry, West Virginia, she just received a new flag today. She was not at home, but family members graciously accepted a new flag on her behalf. I asked about their magnificent flag pole and I was told her husband put it up years ago. Thank you, Naomi!

Naomi
Harpers Ferry, West Virginia

July 4, 2012

Happy Birthday, America!

I made it to the Vietnam Veterans Memorial today. It was not an easy journey; I left my campground and took the Amtrak into D.C., then I took a cab to "The Wall." The only problem is the National Independence Day Parade made it difficult for my cabbie to get me close to my destination. He dropped me off at 13th and I needed 23rd. I walked like a determined woman on a mission.

When I came around the corner and saw the wall, I began sobbing. As I tried to walk towards the wall, my sobbing became uncontrollable as all my emotions came forward. I had to stop and turn around, that is when I noticed a beautiful American flag. I stopped at the flag and proudly said the Pledge of Allegiance with my hand over my heart.

I took a deep breath and re-entered the area of the wall and cried some more. It was hard to believe that so many gave their life for our freedom; true patriots!

When I got to the middle of the wall I placed a photo of John and his buddy Colin (they enlisted together in the Navy on the same day and always wanted to go to the wall together) at the base of the wall. I placed the framed photo and laid an American flag across their photo; they finally made it to the Vietnam Veterans Memorial together!

I sat for a little while and cried some more. I had a woman come up to me and offer me some tissues. After a little more time passed I felt a sense of relief; I knew at that time I could survive.

Comments
Cathy: Bless you, dear Annie. I KNOW John and Colin are smiling down at you right now. You did a good thing. Brave and courageous. Peace.

The Vietnam Wall from across the lawn.

Vietnam Memorial flagpole

I stopped here and said the Pledge of Allegiance.

John and Colin are finally at the Vietnam Memorial Wall.

Comments

Lynette: thank you for sharing this Gale. It's beautiful and inspiring and VERY EMOTIONAL!!!!!

Doug: Gail I can't tell you how much this means to us Thank you from the bottom of my heart! (*Doug is a son of Colin and his wife, Jenny.*)

Lynette: CRYING!!!!!!!!!

Lynette: But tears of JOY!

Jennifer: All my love to them both

Holly: Gale - today was the first day in years I've seen Doug so emotional when talking of his dad. He was so happy and extremely appreciative of what you have done! What they were unable to make happen. You did! You are an amazing inspiration and our family is forever thankful to you for helping to keep Colin's memory alive and providing yet another story that we can all share with the pride that exudes from each one of us that are honored enough to have McIntosh as our last name.

Jennifer: Again and again Gale Thank You

The back of the photo I left at the wall had both Colin's and John's obituaries on it.

Colin McIntosh

A memorial service will be held Sept. 10 for Colin John Pitts McIntosh of Eugene, who died Sept. 5 of prostate cancer. He was 56.

McIntosh was born Oct. 8, 1948, in British Columbia, to Charles and Vivian Pitts McIntosh. He and his wife, Jennifer, were married Nov. 11, 1970, in Huntington Beach, Calif.

He served in the Navy on the USS Constellation, including service in the Vietnam area. He held a bachelor's degree in construction management and building inspection. He had worked as a self-employed contractor, as an operations manager of parking structures for Diamond Parking and as a manager for National Car Rental. He also had worked for the Oregon Employment Department.

He enjoyed spending time with his family, motorcycles, collecting die cast cars, working on cars and restoring classic cars. He belonged to the Veterans of Foreign Wars.

Survivors include his wife; three sons, Andrew McIntosh and Douglas McIntosh, both of Springfield, and Johnny Brewer of Portland; a daughter, Meghan McIntosh of Eugene; and four grandchildren.

John E. Wilkison IV

John E. Wilkison IV, 62 of Chelan, Wash., passed away on the beautiful North Cascade Highway on Nov. 7, 2010.

He was driving eastbound around 8:37 a.m. when his vehicle went off the road to the left and rolled down an embankment before coming to rest on its top, the Washington State Patrol said. Wilkison, who wore a seatbelt, died at the scene.

He was born on April 15, 1948 to John and Marion Wilkison of Ashtabula Ohio. John proudly served his country in Vietnam as part of the U.S. Navy MCB5. He was a lifetime member of the Veterans Foreign Wars, and very active in his local community organizations.

John was passionate about his country and loved riding his Harley. He rode to live, and lived to ride.

John is survived by his wife Gale Wilkison of 26 years, and ex-wife Carol Springer. He is also survived by his son J. Eric Wilkison and daughter-in-law Sara; two grandchildren: Alexander and Tessa-Lynn of Portland, Ore.; son Joseph Wilkison of Bellingham Wash., and daughter Sierra Wilkison of Spokane, Wash.

At the Vietnam Memorial Wall.

July 5, 2012

While I was in line to board the Amtrak back to Harpers Ferry, West Virginia yesterday, I got a phone call from KREM 2 News. They did a follow up interview with me on the phone. See Chapter 5.

July 5, 2012

My day started with good intentions. First I sent my daughter-in-law Sara a happy birthday message via Facebook, did some laundry, went grocery shopping, got gas, filled the propane tank in the van and headed out toward Greenbelt, Maryland. Once I got to Greenbelt, I had planned to drive around looking for tattered flags, but after making two wrong turns on the Parkway (that's what they call a highway here), the drive took me twice as long as planned and I should have been ticketed for not knowing how to navigate the Parkway! (Yes, I used my navigation system, I just wasn't fast enough.) So I'm here at the campground in the shade of the trees and I am not leaving! Tomorrow I head east to hopefully cooler weather and to give away two flags.

Comments

Luana: Just relax girl, things sound a little hectic today!!

Jody: You are amazing and brave and a wonderful writer! We are loving following you.

Karen: Be safe rest up and hit it hard Friday!

July 6, 2012

Good morning, Greenbelt, Maryland.

It's a beautiful 77 degrees this morning with an expected high of 98 degrees, but I'm headed east toward the Atlantic Ocean! Sunrise today was at 5:48. I'm in my 16th state and have traveled 2,846.2 miles.

July 6, 2012

Ron, Vietnam Veteran, Army.

Berlin, Maryland

Ron and Linda
Berlin, Maryland

Comments

Linda: Thank you so much for stopping by our house and presenting us with this beautiful flag. Ron said to tell you that although his country had failed him and other Viet Nam vets, he has never failed his country. Ron served two tours in Viet Nam. My first husband served on tour with the 4th Infantry Division in Viet Nam and died at the age of 31 from the effects of Agent Orange. This flag pole and our house belonged to my father, a marine veteran who served in the Pacific on the Marshall Islands in WWII. He built this house and wanted the flag pole front and center, so proud a man he was. He never saw his new home or the flag pole that Ron had installed for him. Our granddaughter Becky is a new airman serving proudly in the US Air Force. We are a family of veterans and proud of it. Thank you so much for honoring us. I wish I had been here to meet you. Keep up the good work!! Spread the Patriotism!!!

Debra: What a wonderful tribute!

Maureen: More affirmations that you're exactly where you're supposed to be. It must feel great that you're following the path you're destined to follow.

Cathy: blessings all over this family, Lord.

Sandra: How wonderful, Gale. The joy you are spreading by sharing a flag to those in need continues to open up "our" eyes as well to all the wonderful patriotic people in this nation!

Catherine: Thank you....God bless your family

July 7, 2012

Another exciting day for me; early this morning I found the home of Julie, Ken and their son Jackson in Bishopville, Virginia.

Ken was not at home, but I had a chance to chat with Julie and Jackson as I put up their new flag. Jackson will be attending sixth grade next year and I told him that I work at an elementary school. They both recited the Pledge of Allegiance with me and posed for a photo in front of their new flag.

Next, I headed south to Virginia Beach, Virginia. Today may have been the hottest day in this eight-day heat spell (all eight days hitting 100 degrees). The heat index was 109 degrees today. I stopped often for solace in any air-conditioned place I could find.

But the most magnificent thing I did today was to cross the Chesapeake Bay Bridge-Tunnel. It measures 17.6 miles from shore to shore, it has two-mile long tunnels, two bridges and four man-made islands, and it was spectacular. When I arrived in Virginia Beach, I immediately went to First Landing State Park only to find they had no available sites for the night, so I got a day pass and went swimming in the Atlantic Ocean! I'm still searching for a place to spend the night. I would really be happy if a storm came through to cool thing off.

Jackson and Julie
Bishopville, Maryland

After I paid the $12 toll to cross the Chesapeake Bay Bridge-Tunnel, I was asked to pull to the side and turn off my propane bottle. This was the first hint that this was going to be an exciting ride. I was mesmerized by this magnificent man made feat.

As I crossed the bridges I honked my horn and hollered at the fishermen, and as I went through the tunnels my knuckles turned white as I gripped the steering wheel to hold my van in its narrow lane. Chesapeake Bay Bridge was one of the highlights of my trip!

Before my trip was over I had suffered heat exhaustion three times. I found that baby Pedialyte would work to rehydrate me. In the evenings I would sit on the step of my van, doors open, drinking a cocktail of Pedialyte and ice. The third time I had heat exhaustion, besides the usual symptoms, I started getting the chills and knew this was not good. I remember walking unbalanced and seeing stars as I went to the back of a Wal-Mart, where the baby items are, to get a Pedialyte fix. Since that time I always carried an extra bottle with me.

July 9, 2012

Good morning, Ocracoke Island! The cool breeze last night was blissful; I slept wonderfully. I wasn't able to update yesterday for lack of a good internet signal, but yesterday was another amazing day. I traveled south from Virginia Beach to the Outer Banks, and on the way I found Suzanne from Powell's Point, North Carolina. I gave her a new 3x5 American flag and replaced six smaller flags she had as a border to her front door. Thank you, Suzanne!

After I left Suzanne's home, I headed to the Wright Brothers National Memorial. It was another hot day, but I went and explored; fascinating.

Along the way, many people tried to pay me for the flags. I always tell them the flags are free. I try to tell them that John wanted to give away the flags and to accept money would be against what he wanted. On two occasions, individuals placed money in my hand and insisted (firmly) that I take it. And for those two, I did take the monetary donation.

Suzanne
Powells Point, North Carolina

Wright Brothers Memorial

After traveling through Kitty Hawk, Kill Devil Hills and the Nags Head area, I took the Ferry to Ocracoke Island, where I spent the night. Ocracoke Campground is my new happy place in life, quiet and slow paced. Today I will meet John's cousin Anita for the first time.

Once I left the mainland on the free ferry to Ocracoke Island, it felt like I had been transported in time back to a day when life was slower and you had time to stop and smell the flowers. I was very impressed with Ocracoke Island.

Camping on Ocracoke Island.

July 9, 2012

Today is my 30th day on the road, 4,480.0 miles. Does mean I'm halfway done, or halfway there? I prefer to have my cup half full.

I left Ocracoke Island and gave away my first flag of the day to Margaret and Brian of Newport, North Carolina. Brian is retired from the Marines, and let me tell you that man can tie a knot. Brian was in the house recovering from surgery and I tried very hard to untie the knot to put up the new flag. Unfortunately, I was unable to get this Marine's knot undone. I ended up leaving the flag with Margaret for Brian to put up later. The flag and pole was a Christmas gift for Margaret!

Comments

Cathy: blessed indeed. I agree.

Margaret: Wanted to thanks again for the American flag. Brian did get the flag up. And he said even he had a time getting the string untied. Thanks again for what you are doing. You are truly a Patriot. I'm surprised Bill O'Reilly hasn't had you on his show. Be careful out there.

A little later when I was in Cedar Point, North Carolina, I found the home of Sandra. She shared that she lost a son. We talked about loss and healing. Thank you, Sandra; your words helped me. When I asked Sandra why she flew the American flag, she stated that she was very, very blessed to be born in the United States.

Sandra
Cedar Point, North Carolina

When I first met Sandra, I told her my story and why I'm giving away American flags. I told her about John. Sandra shared her story about the loss of her son with me - he was just a little boy when he died - and we both cried. We talked about grief and healing.

I told her that this trip was part of my healing. She told me that she created a scrapbook to help with her healing. What Sandra does not know is that this day was a major turning point for me and *my* healing, thanks to her.

Thank you, Sandra, for sharing your story with me. I hope talking about your son with me helped you as much as it helped me. Thank you.

I contacted Sandra after I got home and asked if I could share her story. She sent me this:

> "Britt Loftin Riddick was born May 19, 1978 in Raleigh, NC. He was my only son. The summer of 1989 he went to our small hometown store to put air

in his bicycle tire and got hit by a car and sadly died at Duke Hospital in Durham, NC 26 hours later.

He was an old man in a little boy's body. He was the light of my life. He was smart, loving, very intelligent and had a delightful sense of humor and a love for life. He never saw a stranger. He insisted on helping every homeless person we saw. He could even tell you the personal story of one local man who had taken up in our small town and lived in the basement of the courthouse on cold nights.

"When asked by doctors at Duke about donating his organs, I knew if I could ask Britt he would insist. Britt died of a head injury. By donating his organs, seven lives were prolonged. Twenty-three years later it is my prayer that these people still live and are enjoying life as much as Britt did.

"The day 'Annie' knocked on my door and asked to replace our American flag and began to tell me what she did and about her husband's accident, I felt the strongest desire to share some of the things I know about grief and healing with her. I told her about the scrapbook I made about Britt and his life and how healing it had been. With every page and every story I relived and celebrated the fun we had on the day it was taken.

"After about 10 pictures I began to remember all the good things his life had brought to my own life, and it dulled the horrible day of the accident. The good outweighed the bad. I also told her the more she talked about her husband, the duller the pain would become because she was setting it free. I watched her via Facebook distribute those flags and carry out her husband's dream.

"When we lose a loved one to a sudden tragic accident, I feel we must go back and reconstruct in our minds the events that led up to that moment. If we look deeply enough we will see all the signs God gives us. And in my case, viewing death as a Christian I now rejoice knowing where my Britt is and that I will see him again one day. If we allow a tragedy to destroy us, then the person's life we have lost holds no meaning. The devil wins. But if we look past our pain and grief and we can help just one person heal, losing our loved one's life takes on new meaning.

"Now, 23 years later, by me sharing a very short version of my loss with a kind stranger performing a random act of kindness I have once again had the privilege to introduce Britt. He will always be with me. I had him in the flesh for 11 years and I will always have him in my heart. John will always remain in the hearts of those who knew and loved him, too.

"Every time I see an American flag, I think of Annie and John. I fly my flag because I was blessed to be born in a free country. I didn't choose where I was born; none of us do. We should never take our freedom for granted nor forget those who defend it."

July 10, 2012

Good morning! Yesterday I arrived in Hubert, North Carolina, home to John's cousin, Anita. John talked of his cousin often, and finally I got to meet her in person. We talked about, well just about everything. She told me many stories of John and his childhood and of their families.

Annie and Cousin Anita.

July 10, 2012

Charlie has been adopted by Carrie! Carrie is Anita's adult daughter. Thank you, Carrie.

I started Charlie from a seed early in 2012. His seed came from a Mortgage Lifter plant I had last year. I nourished and loved him for many months until I realized he needed to get out of my extremely hot van.

July 10, 2012

The heat has finally let up; two nights in a row with bearable temperatures, thank goodness. Today I left Hubert, North Carolina and headed to Elizabethtown, but I was unable to complete a side mission.

I traveled west and found the home of David, in Atkinson, North Carolina. I don't think David fully understood that the flag was free and that I was completing a quest set forth by my husband. When he agreed to accept the flag I had to climb up a ladder onto the roof of his garage to replace the tattered one.

When I asked David why he flew the American flag, he said because he is "proud to be American" and wished more people would fly the American flag every day. Thank you, David, for accepting the new flag.

David
Atkinson, North Carolina

July 10, 2012

Does anyone have a question for me? Maybe one about John, myself, or my trip.

Comments

Barbara: Is this something that you may do again?

Robyn: I don't have a question but think it is amazing what you are doing. Thank you so much for sharing this adventure with us and for standing tall and sharing your American pride!!! As we say in the Army.....hoooaah!

Annie Amerika 2012: I would love to do it again.

Annie Amerika 2012: Robyn, thanks for the shout out...I'm glad to have met so many other proud Americans.

Mariah: Have you found the patriotism you were hoping throughout our country or have you been disappointed?

Annie Amerika 2012: Oh Mariah, I found it alive and well in the U.S. Today I had people honking; giving me the thumbs up, it's amazing. However, I did have one man in Virginia Beach ask me if I sold ice cream.

Jodi: Your amazing! Just sayin

Der Biermann: Climbing up on folks roofs! LoL ... What would John say?

Der Biermann: ...PS: I agree w/Jodi there...

Annie Amerika 2012: Climbing roofs for patriotism... John would say go for it.

July 11, 2012

Today I head to the Charlotte area to visit Mariah and Skye, daughter and grandson to my friend, Teresa. Teresa was the maid of honor at our wedding, and has remained a true friend and confidante throughout all these years.

July 12, 2012

Yesterday I headed towards South Carolina, the 19th state I visited on my journey,

When I arrived in Charlotte the first thing I did was met with David Kernodle from www.news14.com. David rode along with me as did Mariah, Arielle, and Skye as I combed the area looking to give away flag number 41.

Mariah spotted a tattered flag. We pulled in and I met Maurice from Matthews, North Carolina. He was in the Army and thinks everyone should fly a flag. Maurice told me he had been battling prostate cancer and recently found out that the cancer had spread throughout his body. I put a new flag up for him, said the Pledge of Allegiance, and was on my way.

I took David back to his news truck and headed to my "home for the night" when I spotted another tattered flag. At this home was Simon, who is retired from the Air Force and also lives in Matthews.

As I was changing out Simon's flag, I felt some stinging in my feet. I looked down and realized I was standing on a red ant pile. OUCH!

From there, I went with Mariah and Arielle to the Dire Wolves clubhouse. I presented Waya with a new Annin American flag to fly, and I shared my story with them. From there we went to Tumble Weeds and I met CW and Jane. CW is a Patriot Guard Rider, and he presented me with two tattered flags, one flag he flew for 20 missions and the other flag was just flown today in honor of the fallen airmen who came home to Charlotte. I presented CW with a new flag to fly on further missions. Thank you, CW.

Jane, Annie and CW

Maurice's new flag.
Matthews, North Carolina

Jeffers Street kids with their new flags.

Simon
Matthews, North Carolina

Comments

Alene: You are such an amazing woman! I am so grateful you have touched my life! I wish you safe travels! Stay in touch!

Mariah: Supercalifragilisticexpialidocious!!!! Totally made up word, yet I find it appropriate for the experience that I had the opportunity to share yesterday!! A taste of child hood memories and home made me want to spend a zillion more days with one of the most amazing women I have had the pleasure of having in my life! An inspiration all of my life with her kindness and heart, Gale "Annie" continues to motivate me. Annie Amerika 2012, known to me almost all my life as John and Gale Wilkison, stopped for a visit and to present a flag to the Dire Wolves MC yesterday and with her brought an experience I am sure to never forget. While in the area she replaced flags for two unsuspecting home owners, presented a new flag to the Dire Wolves MC and exchanged a new flag with CW Smith for one that has been in over 20 missions and another that was only flown once to honor our fallen airman who came home to Charlotte. Special thanks to you all! I sat in the back of her van while she did an interview with Channel 14 news and listened to her excitement when she talked about what she is doing. This trip is in honor of her late husband but her heart is filled with as much patriotism as he was! I heard her tell the story of his death and cried as I have never heard it before, but my tears were not of sadness but happiness for the peace that this is bringing to her heart, at the joy that she has found in what they had together and that it wasn't allowing her to get stuck in life, that she has found the road to healing. We met a man that couldn't walk to the flag pole. She replaced it because he was ill but he stood and watched her raise it while he talked about how happy his wife would be that it had been replaced. I saw the amazement in his eyes when she refused to take any money, he truly couldn't believe that she did it out of the kindness of her heart and we left with him smiling like she had just given him the sun. I am so honored that she allowed us to be a part of this experience yesterday. I watched her stand in front of a group of people and talk about her life with John and saw the smiles on their faces as she shared with them their life together in a way that she had yet to be able to. So many more things I can say about my yesterday with Annie Amerika 2012! You are an amazing human being; I love you and pray for you on your journey every day. John, I know would be so proud. I can hear him saying "That's my girl" (except I secretly think he would use a word I can't write on Facebook). Love you always, Mariah

July 12, 2012
I am headed into the Great Smoky Mountains National Park to a campground that is isolated. I probably will not

have a cell connection to write a post tonight, but today the temperature has been in the upper 70s and the roads smooth. Beautiful!

Tomorrow I head to Fairfield Glade, Tennessee to visit my Aunt Grayce and Uncle Walt.

July 13, 2012

Glorious day, Thursday was! I headed into the Great Smoky Mountain National Park, 11 miles up twisted clay packed single lane roads until I came to Cataloochee Campground. I camped along the Cataloochee River and fished, it was a cool misty afternoon, perfect night for a campfire. The cool air was welcoming from 100-plus degrees just a few short days ago. My campground hosts were Margaret and Phil; they were very generous and gave me some firewood. This morning before I left I filled my two water jugs with some fresh Smoky Mountain well water. I did not give away a flag yesterday, so today I will be looking extra hard.

July 13, 2012

Today I stopped in Pigeon Forge, Tennessee; very touristy and not many homes. I guess I was looking for Dolly to be walking around singing a song. Anyway, today was one of those days I drove for hours looking to give away a flag. It was just one of those days. Thank goodness I gave away four flags on Wednesday. I stopped in three towns and tried to give away a flag. One time I saw a tattered flag up on the hill, it seemed to be in someone's back yard. I drove for 45 minutes and could not find the house. Disappointed, I left.

Tonight I am at my Aunt Grayce and Uncle Walt's home in Fairfield Glade, and tomorrow it's on to Memphis.

I did stop today in Knoxville to see the world's largest Rubik's Cube!

July 14, 2012

Last night, my aunt and uncle spoiled me. I got caught up on laundry, washed my dishes in hot water, took a long shower and they took me out for a yummy dinner. These two have always had open arms and loving hearts; thank you, Aunt Grayce and Uncle Walt! Also, last night I slept inside a house in a bed. For 34 consecutive nights I have slept in my van! My surroundings were very comfortable and the bed was perfect, yet I woke up at 4 a.m.? Good morning, Fairfield Glade.

July 14, 2012

Hello Columbia, Tennessee! Today I went to the home of Marcia and Terry. Terry was not at home, but I put up a new 4x8 flag for them. I asked Marcia why they flew the American flag and she said "pride". She also said her father was a Korea-era veteran in the Air Force. We talked a bit and she was wondering how long it would take before Terry noticed the new flag. I laughed. Marcia also gave me the directions to Chris and Brenda's home. It was a brick home and they flew the POW/MIA flag, but I was unable find their home.

When I left Marcia and Terry's home, I went just a few doors down to Mary's home. I replaced the flag there and asked why she flew the American flag. She said that it was the proper thing to do; she was a proud American and enjoys her freedom. Also, her father-in-law was in World War II. I loved Columbia!

Marcia
Columbia, Tennessee

Mary
Columbia, Tennessee

I stopped in Waynesboro, Tennessee to get some food at their McDonald's. When I went in, a man asked if I was a veteran. I said, "No, but my husband was. Would you like to hear my story?"

There were about 10 "boys" sitting there socializing and I told them my story. They told me they were all war heroes! It seemed most were World War II veterans, because one talked about chasing French women. Another man replied, "But he never caught one." It was so much fun talking to them.

Another thing happened today that I want to talk about. When I turned onto 43 South, I noticed a police escort for a funeral procession. There must have been 100 cars following the hearse, and I started to cry. I didn't cry out of sadness, but it was at that time I realized how blessed I was. I am truly blessed!

To all my Sierra Valley friends, I got behind a cattle truck today and thought of the sights and smells of Sierra Valley.

And my last thought for the day. I think Tennessee is greener in color than Oregon. Tennessee has huge downpours of rain and just like most people in Oregon, they drive the speed limit!

I have found that most drivers in most of the states I traveled through drive at least 5 mph over the speed limit, but in Tennessee and Oregon they only drive the posted speed limit.

July 15, 2012

5,677.8 miles to Graceland!

Good morning, Memphis. Sunrise was at 5:15 a.m. At 7 a.m. it was 67 degrees, warm with overcast.

Today, I tour Graceland. Thank you Joe and Sierra.

July 15, 2012

The work I do is not about me. This is why I use the moniker Annie Amerika. Giving away flags is about my husband John, patriotism and having pride in our wonderful country.

Elvis Presley
United States Army

July 16, 2012

Yesterday, I played tourist and went to Graceland and visited all things Elvis. I had a wonderful time.

Today I drove around numerous meticulously manicured neighborhoods for hours and I didn't see one single American flag. I'd like to think that there must be a regulation within the city, because I don't want to believe that there would be no patriotic people in Memphis!

Tomorrow I leave the Memphis area and head west into Arkansas, then back east toward Tupelo, Mississippi, and then south. I'll try to give away two flags tomorrow.

July 17, 2012
Mississippi

My day started with a stop at the Tunica Visitors Bureau, where I talked with Aimee. She suggested some areas in town where I might find tattered flags. Tunica residents should be proud of themselves, because after an hour I could not find one tattered flag.

I stopped at *The Tunica Times* and talked to Brooks, as Aimee suggested. Brooks and I talked about my journey and she took some photos. Hopefully I'll have another newspaper article.

I headed south on the "Blues Highway" (Route 61) and stopped at three more towns. (You probably should know that I drive at least an hour when I enter a town.)

I was disappointed by not finding one single flag. None. No small ones, no big ones, no fresh ones, no tattered ones; none in all three towns. Had I failed to give away a flag two days in a row? Then I thought about the last three towns I was in. I thought about the poverty, poverty like none I have seen before in the United States. I don't consider this day a failure, just a glimpse into the real world of Mississippi. Thank you, Mississippi, for teaching me a valuable lesson this summer.

I stopped in Vicksburg and toured the Vicksburg National Military Park and Cemetery. I traveled the nine miles in the park to see the actual place where the Union met with the Confederates, and Grant's Canal was huge. Even if you're not a history buff, this will excite you.
6,024.4 miles, 21 states, 39 days.

This is the site of the American Civil War Battle of Vicksburg waged from May 18 to July 4, 1863. The park includes 1,325 historic monuments and markers, 20 miles of historic trenches and earthworks, and 144 emplaced cannons. This Military Park exudes history.

July 18, 2012
Fifty-five years ago today, my mother gave birth to her first child: a determined, tenacious daughter.

My first birthday

Comments

Lisa: Happy Birthday, Annie Gale! Have a wonderful day as you bless so many more people! God be with you!
Debra: Happy birthday...hope you have a great day and kudos to your mom for such a great daughter!

Claudia: Happy Happy Birthday! Here's to new challenges and adventures! Have a great day!
Grayce: I remember it well! You were an adorable tot and an admirable woman.
Sandra* Yes, I think determined and tenacious does describe you! I too have a picture of me in a "playpen" very similar to yours! Happy Birthday to You! I am so glad you have family to spend it with!!!! Enjoy.

July 18, 2012
Yellow Pine, Alabama is on the map.

Today I found the home of Azalea in Yellow Pine. I told her my story, and she told me her husband died 10 years ago. She joined me in putting up the new flag, but the rope crumbled and broke in my hands.

She called her grandson and nephew; they brought over a ladder and grandson Aladdin put up the new rope. I put up the new American flag and by this time, several relatives had gathered. They all recited the Pledge of Allegiance with me.

It was my pleasure to meet Azalea with her warm heart, her grandson Aladdin, her nephew Tyler, her daughter Maggie and her cousin Barbara. When I asked Azalea why she flies the American flag, she said her husband always flew the flag, and now she flies it to honor him. Azalea, thank you for my birthday gift!

Everyone I met on the road has a special place in my heart, but Azalea helped heal my heart. I enjoyed talking to her about the loss of our spouses. She said because the flagpole was her husband's idea, she continued with it. We laughed as she said she still does what her husband told her to do, even 10 years after his death. I would love to meet with Azalea and her family again one day. She was a sweetheart.

Azalea's new flag
Shown with Tyler and Aladdin
Yellow Pine, Alabama

July 18, 2012

Later I stopped in Citronelle, Alabama, and saw a beautiful tribute to veterans at American Legion Post No. 164. I took a few photos and went inside and introduced myself.

Tonight I am with my sister Maureen in the Mobile, Alabama, area. I love life!

My sister Maureen and I celebrating my Birthday.

What a beautiful tribute to our nation's heroes!

July 19, 2012

Good morning, Spanish Fort, Alabama.

Sunrise today was at 6:02 a.m. Current temperature is 78 degrees (nice), humidity 89 percent (not good).

Today is going to be a busy day, but you will have to check back later to see just what it is.

July 19, 2012

Today at 10 a.m. I met with Boy Scout Troop 177 from Spanish Fort, Alabama, to retire American flags, 34 in all. Also in attendance were Devon Walsh, news anchor for WKRG News 5, and her camera man Arnell Hamilton.

Scout master for the troop is Brian, who coordinated the morning activities with his boys and Devon.

Devon interviewed me first, and then we proceeded with the flag retirement ceremony. It was a touching ceremony, as one boy read about the flag folds and their meanings.

They also took a minute to pray for all service members and for John. I cried as I thought about him.

Two adult members of the troop, both military veterans, accepted the flags and proceeded to retire them with honor. When the ceremony was done, Devon interviewed some of the boys and Arnell took more video for the news story that will most likely air tomorrow at 6 p.m.

I am so blessed to live in such a great country, and to have met these wonderful people of the Gulf area. It was an honor to have met all of you.

Boy Scout Troop 177

Comments

Sandra: I have been so touched by your mission and I pray that God will heal your heart!!! Stay safe. You are a shining example of a true American Patriot!!!!

Maureen: My heartfelt thanks to Brian B. for gathering the troop, and to the other leaders and young men of Boy Scout Troop 177 for carrying out my late brother-in-laws wish. You should all be proud of your exemplary dedication to honor and patriotism. John would have been proud. I sure am...

Pam* As the mom of one of the boys in this picture, I didn't know what today was about until this moment. Thank you, for making our boys a part of your journey and mission.

July 20, 2012

Today's flag went to Steve and Janeen. They live in the Belforest area of Daphne, Alabama. A brand new 3x5 Annin

American flag is now flying on their flagpole in their beautiful front yard.

Janeen was not at home, but Steve proudly accepted the new flag. When I asked him why they flew the American flag, he said it was the right thing to do, so today's patriotism award goes to Steve and Janeen.

Steve
Belforest, Alabama

July 21, 2012

First and only rejection:

My sister Maureen and I headed into Florida to see if we could give away some flags, but didn't find any needing replacement in the areas we drove around. On our way back to Spanish Fort, Alabama, I spotted a tattered flag in the Point Clear area.

I went and knocked on the door and explained to the gentleman my mission. He said no, thank you. I asked if he saw me on TV last night and he said no and no thank you. I asked if he wanted my card to check me out on the Internet, and he said no thank you.

I left his home feeling a bit defeated, but also amazed because I have traveled 6,411 miles before I received my first rejection. I honored his right to reject my flag; after all, this is America!

Comments

Cathy: he probably didn't reject you or your flag....probably just didn't trust you were who you said you were. People are scared these days. Too many door to door people casing our houses so they can come back later and cause trouble. HUGS to you, however. I am sure you did feel like he rejected you. Keep on keepin on. You are doing a good thing. Standing with you with prayers and affection.

Lise: Trust, coming from our neck of the woods we forget that there are others that have spoiled it for the rest of us. Keep up the good work Annie. Don't let this one discourage you. We are all so very proud of you.

Joni: Either that, or he was just a very disagreeable and suspicious person, thinking that there had to be some "catch" to it. I'm so happy that you've gone all this way before your first rejection. I cannot help but think of the 40+ people whose lives were made happier by you and your mission

Jhen: I was wondering about this actually, when and if someone would reject the offer...My theory... He has some sort of personal attachment to this flag. I wouldn't be offended or feel rejection at all. You're doing a great thing but we have to understand that some people just want to be left alone or that perhaps he is proud he has been flying that flag for a loooooong time :)

Robert: I agree Jhen. This is a beautiful Flag. A demonstration of true Patriotism. There is nothing prouder than a tired and worn flag. God bless him.

The day before this rejection, a mass shooting occurred at a Century movie theater in Aurora, Colorado, during a midnight screening of the film "The Dark Knight Rises." A gunman, dressed in tactical clothing, set off tear gas grenades and shot into the audience with multiple firearms, killing 12 people and injuring 58 others, maybe this is why he seemed apprehensive.

"UNNAMED SOLDIER"
Point Clear, Alabama
I have come to realize that this may be the most beautiful flag I have ever seen, one flown proudly and most likely for many years.

July 22, 2012

6,439.5 miles, 23 states.

My 44th day on the road.

78 degrees at 6:15 a.m. Sunrise was at 6:04 a.m., and I headed out early.

546 miles, that is how far I traveled today, and approximately 500 of those miles the view was of cotton and corn fields. Thank you, farmers, for all you do.

My first flag went to James of Alsatia, Louisiana. James told me that when he was in school, it was his job to put up the flag each day. He also stated that he is proud to be an American.

James
Alsatia, Louisiana

My second flag went to Carol and Bill Smith of McGehee, Arkansas. Bill asked me to use his last name. The flag that flies in front of their home was put there by Carol's father, Robert Russell. Robert who was an MP in the military is now deceased.

Bill
McGehee, Arkansas

A third flag went to Bill's neighbor, Raymond. Raymond is an older gentleman.

While I was putting up Bill and Carol's flag, Raymond drove up and said it was about time the military replaced Robert's flag; they had been waiting for someone to show up with a new flag. I tried to explain my journey to him and that I was not with the military, but he didn't seem to hear me. Then he told me he finally took down his flag pole because no one brought him a flag, and then he asked me for a flag. Before I could answer he started talking politics, at which time I asked him, "If I give you a flag, will you put your pole back up?" He said, "Yes, ma'am." I gave him a flag and he was a happy man.

July 23, 2012

Greg and Mari Etta of Enid, Oklahoma, are now flying their new American flag. Greg said that one of the reasons he flies an American flag is because he works for the government. Mari Etta was happy to receive the new flag.

Greg and Mari Etta, Enid, Oklahoma

Comments

Pam: I just wanted to say God Bless You and your travels ...I have tried to get my grandfather's flag for many years now and have been unable to get one but I salute the ones around here in his honor, you are a wonderful person and your husband was a very lucky man...I am honored to be called an American because of people like you ....Thank You and God Bless.

While in Enid, Oklahoma, I visited with my cousin Marjorie and her four children. This is the first time I met her family, and I was truly tickled by the children's kindred spirits and enchanting souls.

**Mikayla, Jack, Eliana and Olivia
Enid, Oklahoma**

July 24, 2012

Yesterday I met Debby, wife of Doug Bergman. Doug is with Cimarron Council No. 474, comprised of approximately 6,500 youth and volunteer Scouters. Debby was able to take four tattered flags for the council. Thank you, Debby!

**Kansas Veterans Cemetery in
Fort Dodge, Kansas**

Lynyrd Skynyrd said, "Ooh ooh, that smell, can't you smell that smell?" I wish I could articulate the smells I have been experiencing over the past 200 miles.

Let's say southwest Kansas should be cattle capitol of the world. I have experienced the smells of cattle in the fields, cattle in the stock yards, cattle being transported by trucks and cattle in the processing plant; the latter producing a smell that I will never forget, but what an experience it has been.

I stopped at a Wal-Mart this evening and they had no trees in the parking lot. I knew I couldn't sleep there in this heat, so I kept driving until I found a campground. The campground had large beautiful trees and there was an awesome breeze.

July 25, 2012

Good morning, Colorado.

I have traveled 7,763.1 miles. I'm in my 28th state. Today is my 47th day on the road.

Sunrise today will be at 5:48 a.m. It is 72 degrees at 5 a.m.

Today I will travel over Wolf Creek Pass at 10,856 feet elevation.

Today's patriotic award goes to Mark and Marian of Alamosa, Colorado. They are truly unsuspecting homeowners, because they were not at home when I knocked on the door but their son Steven was at home and he accepted the flag on their behalf.

What you need to know about Steven is that he has a radiant smile, like a ray of sunshine. He told me that his grandpa was in World War II, his Uncle Matthew is a disabled naval veteran, and his father Mark was an Eagle Scout. Now we know why this family proudly fly's the American flag.

I spent the night in the Durango, Colorado, Wal-Mart parking lot. I walked around the town, the same town that John and I visited on our honeymoon. The narrow gauge train is still available for rides, just as we rode on our honeymoon. I enjoyed reminiscing through this beautiful town.

Comments

Carla: Well, that calls for a song. :-) C. W. McCall "Wolf Creek Pass"

Annie Amerika 2012: John loved that song...

Sara: Eric LOVES that song too - we have played it many times :-) It brings back lots of good memories of his Dad :-)

Steven
Alamosa, Colorado

July 26, 2012

Aurora, Utah's "hidden oasis." I fell in love with this town of less than 1,000 people and found three flags in need of replacement, but my knocks were unanswered. Sometimes it's hard to give away flags during daytime hours. I headed toward Moab, Utah.

Moab, Utah, is home to Clinton and Carlen. Their flag was in desperate need of replacement. I talked with Carlen and she said her husband Clinton is disabled and has not been able to get out and replace the flag.

She stated that Clinton was in the Army, and they had received a flag when their son died. She didn't offer any details and I honored her privacy by not asking any questions. I felt honored to give them a new flag and to be able to put it up for them. I immensely enjoy meeting the people I give flags to. Thank you, Clinton and Carlen.

Clinton and Carlen
Moab, Utah

July 27, 2012
Good morning, Delta, Utah.
Sunrise was at 6:23 a.m. It is 68 degrees at 7 a.m.
Today I will travel to Nevada, my 30th state.
July 27 is my 49th day on the road. I have traveled 8,538.7 miles spreading patriotism.

Comments

Elizabeth: Dear Annie, for nearly 50 days I have enjoyed your travels and your patriotism across our wonderful country. When your journey is finished whatever will I do during my lunch breaks?

Highway 6 across the great state of Nevada should be called America's loneliest highway.

I left Delta, Utah, this morning and headed west on Highway 6. Shortly after leaving I saw this sign: "Next gas 167 miles." I felt good about the drive, since I just got some gas and had a full cup of coffee.

The traveling was slow. I don't go much over 65 mph, and over the summits I average 35 mph. I got a smile on my face when I saw the sign that said Pacific Time Zone.

When I got to Ely, I looked for tattered flags but didn't find any. I left and headed to my destination of Tonopah, Nevada. Then two miles out of Ely, I saw a sign that said, "Next gas 96 miles," so I turned around and filled up my tank to be on the safe side.

I spent six hours driving through some barren country, but this is where I want to thank Meat Loaf's "Bat out of Hell" for being my constant companion.

Comments

Brad: Welcome to Nevada, Annie! Since you're in my state, I'll take this opportunity to tell you my flag story. I teach at school named after a former governor, Kenny Guinn (R). When I noticed that our school's flag was looking pretty beat up with age and our bright, desert sun, I called the governor (the one for whom my school is named, who was in office at the time), and I asked a staffer if the governor would like to donate a new flag... one that had been flown over the Capitol in Carson City. My request was denied, but we managed to pull some money out of our student-generated funds account to buy a new flag. May the rest of your travels be safe and rewarding, and thanks for being a great American!

July 27, 2012

Minnie's parents immigrated to the United States from Yugoslavia before the 1920s and became American citizens. Her parents always flew the American flag and so does she, because "We believe in America."

Minnie told me that the tattered flag she flies daily was from the Auxiliary, which she is a part of. She also shared that she was born in the house next door, and then she laughed and said, "I guess I didn't make it too far."

Minnie
Tonopah, Nevada

July 28, 2012

I want to give a shout out to the three girls I met at Mono Lake. I hope you go back to Germany with wonderful thoughts of the United States.

You see I stopped to make breakfast at a beautiful rest stop on Mono Lake in California. While I was eating my breakfast, the three girls walked by and asked me a few questions about my van. We chatted for a bit and they told me they were headed back to Germany after being in the United States for one year, but before they head back they are touring to see the sights.

July 28, 2012

Today is my 50th day on the road, and this morning I entered California, the 31st state of my trip.

The first flag today went to Pam of Bridgeport, California. Pam answered the door wearing a patriotic shirt and I got a smile on my face.

Her tattered flag was flying upon a tree pole 30 feet in the air; very impressive. She accepted the new American flag, but we were unable to get the old one down; it seemed stuck. She said she had someone who could fix it, but they were not at home at the moment. I left a new flag for them to put up later this afternoon.

Pam and I talked about why she flies the American flag and she told me, with tears in her eyes, "Because our guys are still over there fighting for us." She talked about her three boys and their father. She said he was in the Marines and went to Vietnam four times! I want to thank you, Pam, for telling me why you are patriotic and fly the American flag every day.

Pam
Bridgeport, California

The second flag today went to Carol of Bridgeport, California.

Carol is a recent widow, having been married to Henry for 59 years. She told me Henry was in the Air Force and every day he put up the flag and every night took it down. I told her John did the same thing.

I cried as Carol told me about her husband. She talked about him the same way I talk John, as if he was still standing beside her. John and Henry seemed to be alike in many ways. Both men were proud to have served their countries, and both men put up and took down the American flag daily. She said that Henry even took the flag down when it got windy or rained. I told her John did the same thing. As Carol shared her story with me, I felt my healing process continuing.

She said the Pledge of Allegiance with me and gave me a hug before I left. Thank you, Carol, for accepting the new American flag. Henry would be proud!

Carol, Bridgeport, California

I met with my longtime friend Carlen today, along with her son and daughter-in-law. They drove to Bridgeport from the Sonora, California area to spend a little time with me.

I enjoyed seeing her; it had been about six years since we last saw each other.

Carlen and myself in Bridgeport, California.

July 28, 2012

This afternoon I gave away my third American flag to Ron and his lovely lady, Rita. Ron lives in Walker, California.

I was driving down 395 and almost missed the fact that his flag was tattered because the entire outside of his house was decorated in patriotic décor. Ron told me that his place looks like this all the time and it wasn't just decorated for the Fourth of July.

Ron also said he was not in the military but was patriotic, and showed me his patriotic Harley. They also showed me numerous other items that were red, white and blue.

I asked why they fly the American flag, and before Rita spoke she had tears coming down her face. She said of the flag, "It makes me cry because it's so beautiful."

Ron and Rita may be the most patriotic people I have met on the road.

> This was sent to me and I felt that everyone needed to see this.... Annie - Cool thing you are doing. Ron is my Dad. He called me in tears so thrilled to have met you and have the honor of flying one of you flags. He said you were "bitchen" AKA Super Cool. Thanks for all you are doing and know that John is so very proud of you for going the distance.

Ron's patriotic bike.

Ron and Rita
Walker, California

July 29, 2012
Good morning, Topaz Lake, Nevada!
I have traveled 9,102 miles to see your morning sun.

Sunrise was at 5:59 a.m., and the temperature at 6:20 a.m. is a crisp 42 degrees.

Topaz Lake, Nevada

Today I stopped in at Tires Plus in Reno, Nevada.
I asked for an oil change, tire rotation and a brake inspection. Troy was my mechanic, and what a wonderful mechanic he is. Thank you, Troy, for your time and expertise. I also stopped at The Flag Store in Sparks, Nevada, and wanted to say hello to Martin, but they were closed. The Flag Store is where purchased all my flags. Thank you, Martin and staff.

July 29, 2012
Elaine and Bob of Cold Springs, Nevada, are the recipients of a new American flag. I talked with Elaine, and

she said her husband is a veteran of the Korean War. He was in the Navy.

When I asked her why she flew the American flag, she said because of "patriotism, it's a symbol of what we have." Thank you Elaine, for accepting the new American flag on behalf of my husband John and myself.

Elaine and Bob
Cold Springs, Nevada

This afternoon I found the home of Dee in Cold Springs, Nevada.

Dee was not at home, but her respite worker/personal care assistant, Mary, was there. Mary felt that Dee would be happy to receive the new American flag.
I put up the new flag, and as always said the Pledge of Allegiance. Mary told me Dee was an advocate for shaken baby syndrome and gave me the following site to look up, and this is what I found. "Dee K. carries the torch forward to educate the community to 'Never Shake a Baby.'"

I am honored to give Dee a new American flag.

Comments

Dee: Annie, I could not believe the wonderful surprise today when I came home from church. I am amazed at what you are doing! May God bless and keep you safe. You are a true AMERICAN!! Love the Klymman's

Dee
Cold Springs, Nevada

July 30, 2012

I'd like you to meet Barbara from Loyalton, California. Today I gave Barbara a new American flag to fly above her Army flag. Barbara told me her son Lang is in the Army serving at Fort Lewis. When I asked her if that is why she flies the American flag, she said that she flew the flag before he went into the Army and they have been flying the American flag since September 11, 2001. So today's patriotic salute goes to Barbara and her son Lang. Thank you, Barbara, for accepting the new 3x5 American flag.

Barbara
Loyalton, California

July 31, 2012

Today I traveled throughout Sierra Valley, California. I journeyed through Loyalton, Portola and Delaker, but was unable to find any tattered flags. John and I lived in this scenic Sierra Valley, and it was comforting traveling around seeing the beautiful valley again.

I ran into a few people I knew, Jasper and Brodie in Loyalton and Susan in Portola. It was comforting.

Tomorrow I will be speaking at Loyalton Senior Center, telling everyone about my patriotic travels.

August 1, 2012

Today I ate a delicious lunch at Loyalton Senior Center, which was accompanied by wonderful conversations with the valley's local residents.

I started my presentation at 12:30 p.m., with over 40 people in attendance. I talked about John, patriotism, my travels giving away American flags to unsuspecting homeowners and healing.

After my presentation I spent time sharing stories, laughing and crying with old friends and new. It was a special day of healing for me. I feel vivacious and alive; thank you, Loyalton.

Comments

Shirley: I loved getting to see you today!! You are awesome!!
Barbara: I feel so honored to have gotten to listen to you speak; I am so proud of your travels and all you've done. I know John is proud of you too!!
Cathy: me too. I love healing with good friends.

Here I am showing them how tattered some flags get.

While I was in Sierra Valley I stayed with my longtime friend, Juli, and her family.

Danny, Juli, Annie, Jillian and Jess.

August 2, 2012

Today stared out rough for me as I traveled for hours up and down the streets of Burney, McCloud, Shasta and Weed. I got to know the area so well that I felt like I could have been a tour guide.

I started feeling a little disappointed because I was unable to find tattered American flags that needed replacement. Then I realized that the beautiful new American flags I saw flying everywhere was a sign of patriotism, and my heart was joyful.

I traveled up Interstate 5 and I saw a tattered flag off to the side of the Interstate. I took the next exit and found the home of Eddie in Grenada, California. Eddie is one of those people whose eyes twinkle when he talks, and he made me smile. We chatted and Eddie told me he works for Grenada Elementary School, and he was honored that I chose his home for a new flag.

When I asked him why he flew the American flag he said, "I love this nation." He felt that everyone should get a chance to go to Washington, D.C. to see what this country is founded on and what it's about. Eddie is shown in this photo with his new 4x6 American flag, Mount Shasta and her snow-swept peaks are featured in the background.

Comments
Linda: Oh what a beautiful bit of country Eddie lives in. Annie you are a gracious and wonderful woman.

Barbara: I agree with Eddie. Everyone should travel to Washington D.C. to see our nation's history!
Tammy: Annie: Eddie wants to thank you for your visit and thanks you for the honor to fly your flag.

Eddie, Grenada, California

August 3, 2012

Good morning, Hornbrook, California.

9,615 miles, 56 days, 31 states (one left), and 62 flags given away.

Its 55 degrees at 6:47 a.m. Sunrise today was at 6:06 a.m.

I arrived this afternoon at the home of my beautiful, intelligent and charming grandchildren, Alex and Tessa-Lynn – oh, and their parents, Eric and Sara. I spent some time this afternoon looking for tattered American flags, but was unable to find any.

Tomorrow I'm headed toward Metzger, Oregon, but in the meantime I'm just being a grandma tonight.

Alex and Tessa-Lynn

August 4, 2012

With 19 flags to give away, my trip to spread patriotism is far from over. I will be home on the afternoon of August 12, which means that I still have eight full days to give away flags.

Today I met a beautiful young woman named Natalia and her son, Markus, in Tigard, Oregon. Natalia came to the United States from Kazakhstan. When I asked Natalia why she flies the American flag, she stated that she is an immigrant from Kazakhstan and being here (United States) has given her opportunities she never dreamed of.

Natalia recited the Pledge of Allegiance with me and I took a photo of Markus holding the small flag I gave him in front of the new 3x5 Annin American flag.

**Markus in front of Natalia's new flag.
Tigard, Oregon**

August 5, 2012
Good morning and happy Sunday, Tigard, Oregon.
At 6:26 a.m. it is 66 degrees. Sunrise was at 6 a.m.
I have driven 9,966.5 miles through 32 states in 58 days.
Today I head to Vernonia and Astoria!
Otto of Seaside, Oregon, is the recipient of a new
American flag. Otto and his friends said the Pledge of
Allegiance with me. Otto was very pleased with his new flag.
When I asked him why he flies the American flag, he stated
that he has been patriotic all his life. He erected his flagpole
on September 12, 2001, the day after the 9/11 attacks.

Comments

Linda: Thank you Annie! It was a pleasure meeting
you and sharing in your journey!

Carey: Awesome! Otto and Cindi are dear friends of mine, and have always been proud and patriotic Americans...

Otto
Seaside, Oregon

August 6, 2012

This afternoon, I found a tattered flag in the well-manicured garden at the home of Dorothy, of Astoria, Oregon.

Dorothy watched as I put up the new 3x5 American flag, and as always I said the Pledge of Allegiance. Dorothy told me her husband, Donald, had retired from the Navy after serving in the Korean and Vietnam conflicts, but he had passed.

I thanked her on behalf of my husband and myself for accepting the new American flag. Her yard was just beautiful; the flowers were in full bloom.

Dorothy
Astoria, Oregon

Steve and Barb of Astoria, Oregon, flew a 5x8 American flag that was slightly tattered. I offered to replace it for them, but unfortunately, the largest flag I had with me was a 4x8, but they accepted my offer of a new flag.

Visiting them was Steve's sister-in-law, Jane, and the children, to whom I also gave small American flags. Everyone joined in saying the Pledge of Allegiance with me.

When I asked Steve why he flew the American flag, he said it is because he is patriotic and wants everyone to know it. They live on the main road in town, and everyone can see their patriotism.

Steve also told me he served in the Army during Vietnam. I thanked Steve for his service to our great nation. Before I left, Barb gave me a hug and thanked me.

Comments
Barb: What a great day! Thank you!

Steve and Barb
Astoria, Oregon

While I was in Astoria I stayed with my childhood friend, Joni, and her husband Brian. Joni and I have known each other since 1967. I had a wonderful time visiting with her and seeing the beautiful sites of Astoria.

I particularly liked the Astor Street Opry Company, where I saw "Shanghaied in Astoria." I also enjoyed a vigorous climb up the Astoria Column.

Me and Joni

August 7, 2012

Sixty days ago I left home to embark on a journey of a lifetime. I took the back roads of our beautiful country to feel and breathe the cultures of rural America.

I have given away 66 flags to this country's most patriotic people - these people have changed my life forever. I have six days remaining of my "Flags for America" sojourn, and I realize it's just the beginning. Although my trip may be ending, my journey is not. I will write a book about this "once in a lifetime" journey.

August 8, 2012

Yesterday, I met two kindred spirits from Colorado at a rest stop. These two women left their homes about the same time I did and they have traveled 11,000 miles. They are taking photos of a rubber duck named "Ducky" at different places all over the country.

They were on their way to Canada on I-5 North. I have not heard from them since this meeting, but hope to one day read about Ducky's journey.

I stayed at my son Joe's house for a few days. I was delighted that he was able to come along with me to give away a flag.

I have not been happy with my van tires that I got in Ohio; if you remember, they would only sell me the manufacturer suggested size. I believe that the size recommended on the side of the door was before the conversion was done which added a lot of weight. So today I went to Les Schwab, my favorite place to buy tires. They recommended a six ply to lift the weight off of the side of the tires. So, on this trip I bought my second set of tires. At least I'm set for a while.

Today I met Veronica, a delightful mother of three. I had driven up and down roads for over an hour and was just about to head back to base camp when I saw a faded, but not tattered, flag flying in Lynden, Washington. I pulled in and found the home of Veronica, Derrick and their three young children.

After I put up the new flag, Veronica and eldest daughter, Kallee, recited the Pledge of Allegiance with me. I asked Veronica why they continued to fly the American flag that the previous owners had left, and she said her husband was in the Air Force for 10 years and participated in Operation Enduring Freedom, the war in Afghanistan. I want to personally thank Derrick for his service to our great nation.

Veronica, Leena and Kallee
Lynden, Washington

August 10, 2012

Good morning, Bellingham, Washington! Happy Birthday Joe.

At 6:33 a.m. it's 50 degrees; great sleeping weather.
Sunrise was at 5:57 a.m. Yearly rain in Bellingham is 20.2 inches.

Sixty-three days on the road, 10,505 miles, 32 states, 69 flags given away. That's more than my original goal of one per day.

Today I'm off to Lynnwood, Washington!

What a glorious day to give away American flags!

My first stop today was at the Boy Scouts of America, Mount Baker area council, where I met Janet. I told Janet about my trip and donated a bag full of tattered flags for the boys. She told me that her husband Norville and son Glen are both veterans, and Glen is the Quartermaster at the Bellingham VFW Post 1585. I want to express my sincere thank you to Norville and Glen for their dedication and service to our country.

When I left Bellingham I headed to Everett, Washington, and found the home of Amanda. Amanda's flag was slightly tattered. I asked to replace it and she agreed. I put up the new flag and said the Pledge of Allegiance with my friend Teresa, then went to the side yard to talk to Amanda.

Visiting Amanda was her cousin Kaytlyn and Kaytlyn's adorable infant son, Benjamin. I asked Amanda why she flies the American flag and she said it was out of respect, and that they have family in the military. Kaytlyn's husband is currently in the Air Force stationed in Oklahoma.

Mom and Joe

Amanda, Kaytlyn and Benjamin
Lynwood, Washington

I stayed in Lynwood with my friend Teresa, who was visiting her friends Jerome and Leree. The company and conversation was wonderful and the food delicious.

Teresa and Annie

August 11, 2012

I traveled 10,744 miles to give Gerry and Dee of Cle Elum a new American flag. I had driven around Cle Elum for a few hours and found six flags in need of replacement, but found no one at home. Who could blame them on this beautiful summer day?

I found Gerry at his home on a dead end street. Dee even asked me how I found them, and I said I literally drive up and down streets looking for tattered flags, even if the sign says dead end.

When I asked why they fly the American flag, Dee told me it was because of all the wonderful freedom we have. Gerry said he was in the Army and is a Vietnam veteran.

Gerry and Dee
Cle Elum, Washington

I will spend my last night on the road with Sue and the good people from West Seattle Fraternal Order of the Eagles 2643 at Eagle Valley Campground.

Sue read about me in the *Quad City Herald*, contacted me and... well, here I am.

I spent the day with Sue and my new friends as we played some interesting games. Thank you for your hospitality.

August 12, 2012

Today as I head home, I will ponder my journey and all the beautiful patriotic people I have met along the way. People, who have changed me forever and helped heal my heart, healed by sharing their stories. Remembering those that made me laugh, and cry. I anticipate temporary sadness when I get home, but my heart will be filled with love and I will never forget just how blessed I am.

Comments

Claudia: Safe journey home. You are indeed blessed and so are all of us for just knowing you.

Lynn: no time for "sadness" ... you've got a book to outline... maps to produce... photos to organize... GET BUSY.!!

Maureen: I would imagine completing your journey would be a little like the day after Christmas, but the gift you gave yourself and everyone you met along the way will last so much longer than a new sweater! Your book will be a lasting memoir of this journey that you can "visit" anytime you feel the need. I am so proud of you sister, for having the strength and conviction to follow your heart, even when others didn't understand the need. I love you!

Juli: I will love you for always. You make this world a better place.

Sandra: I was blessed to have met you!!! Can't wait to read that book!!!!

Jenny: What an amazing trip this has been! You have blessed so many people! So proud of you!!!

Luana: So happy to have you home safe, what a wonderful journey for you and all those you have touched....for me, I can say every time I read a post it was an exciting, emotional journey for me too, I also did a lot of thinking and soul searching.... Thank You Annie from the bottom of my heart!!

4

HOME AGAIN...

I arrived home mid-day on Sunday, August 12. It was a beautiful sunny day and the air was warm.

I went into my cozy home and sat in my recliner for a few minutes, thinking about how blessed I have been, not only on this journey, but in life. How blessed to have met so many patriotic Americans, blessed to have said the Pledge of Allegiance with over 70 people.

Then I realized that I made it; I made the journey of a lifetime. I did not have to sign the title of my van over to a wrecking yard, I did not have to travel back home on a bus. I completed John's mission, the dream of a disabled Vietnam veteran, and I began to cry.

The final facts:
   65 days on the road.
   10,889.4 miles traveled.
   32 states visited.
   70 flags given away.

During my 65-day odyssey, I swam in the Missouri River, Lake Erie, the Atlantic Ocean, the Gulf of Mexico and the Pacific Ocean.

These are the states I traveled through:
Washington, Idaho, Montana, Wyoming, South Dakota, Minnesota, Iowa, Wisconsin, Illinois, Indiana, Michigan, Ohio, Pennsylvania, Virginia, West Virginia, Maryland,

Delaware, North Carolina, South Carolina, Tennessee, Mississippi, Alabama, Florida, Louisiana, Arkansas, Oklahoma, Kansas, Colorado, Utah, Nevada, California and Oregon.

September 9, 2012

Yesterday I met with a few close friends, and we retired two special American flags. These two flags were given to me by CW Smith on July 11, 2012, when I was in North Carolina.

CW is a Patriot Guard Rider from North Carolina. Patriot Guard Riders is a group of riders from across the nation who have an unwavering respect for those who risk their lives for America's freedom and security. Their mission is to attend funeral services of fallen American heroes as invited guests of the family. Each mission has two basic objectives: to show sincere respect for fallen heroes, their families and their communities, and to shield the mourning family and friends from interruptions created by any protestors.

John was a Patriot Guard, having attended two missions, so when CW told me that the first flag he gave me was flown on the back of his motorcycle for 20 missions and the second flag flown that day for one mission, I was honored to accept the flags for retirement. I knew these flags needed special treatment, so I saved them until yesterday.

There were five of us in attendance, so we started by using some of John's ashes and the ashes of the first flag retirement ceremony done on June 10, 2012, to start the fire. We said the Pledge of Allegiance and I read about CW and the Patriot Guard. We joined hands in a circle and my son-in-law Brett, an Eagle Scout, said a prayer. We retired the two flags with honor and dignity.

These two flags represent 21 fallen soldiers; the reality is those flags symbolized someone's child, parent or sibling. They gave their life for our freedom and security!

It seemed fitting to retire these flags at the first campground where I started this journey: Hawk Creek Campground. After the ceremony I got in touch with CW and mailed him one of the charred grommets from the flags he donated. I hear they bring good luck.

Comments

Cathy: Thank you. I send up words and prayers of honor and respect for these men and their friends and family. AND, for John and for you and the others there with you. Blessings and hugs.

Sandra: God Bless you!!!

Michele: what a moving story! Thanks for sharing it with us.

Alene: You continue to inspire people!!! You are on such a great mission! Thankful I got to meet you!

Cw: HONOR..RESPECT..FOR ALL..GREAT JOB....thank you.

5

MEDIA COVERAGE

March 14, 2012
"'Annie Amerika' carries on late husband's dream"
By Jennifer Marshall
Herald Staff Writer

BRIDGEPORT - It's been a little more than a year since her husband, John, was suddenly killed in a rollover accident, and Gale Wilkison plans to honor his memory the best way she knows how - an old-fashioned American road trip, with some community service thrown in.

It had long been John's dream to travel the country with his wife to replace tattered American flags with crisp new ones made in the USA. But having died in November 2010, he never got to take that trip they had finally planned for last year.

"He was a disabled Vietnam veteran, and he had talked about traveling across the country visiting relatives, seeing national parks things like that - but along the way what he wanted to do was replace worn and tattered American flags," Wilkison said, adding that it would have been a free gift to the flag's owner.

The old flags, in turn, would be given to local Boy Scout troops so they could learn the proper flag retirement ceremony.

Now Wilkison is picking up the torch, speaking to area groups and applying for sponsorships for her 8,600-mile journey set to begin June 12.

One of those sponsorships comes courtesy of the Chelan Senior Center, where Wilkison recently gave a presentation about her trip. Other sponsorships so far are by the Veterans of Foreign Wars Post 6853, the Fraternal Order of the Eagles Auxiliary 2218 and Signs Etcetera, owned by Kimberly Gormley of Waterville.

Wilkison and her husband moved to Chelan in May 2010 after his retirement. She has lived in Bridgeport for about five months, working as a paraprofessional at Bridgeport Elementary School.

"My world came upside down," Wilkison said of her husband's death. "We had been together for 30 years. It just - everything changed. So about six months ago, I decided that going around the country and replacing these worn and tattered American flags was not only something that he wanted to do, but something that I really wanted to do."

Wilkison, using the moniker "Annie Amerika," will embark on the trip alone in her 1985 red and gray Chevy van, making a few stops here and there to see family or friends along the way. She plans to take the simple two-lane back roads through small towns and visit the local newspapers and city halls to help find other like-minded patriots who could use a new flag.

Her alias comes from a nickname she was given at a biker rally in Waterville last spring, a benefit for "Kids to the Capitol." The nickname, Annie, came from a group of middle-school age children.

"It's going to be a time of healing for me," she said. "Twenty-seven states, 60 days across the country."

She said the first flag she gives away will be at home right in Bridgeport.

John E. Wilkison IV enlisted in the Navy in December 1966. He served as a Seabee, or construction battalion, helping clear roads for front line troops to get through.

A lifetime VFW member, he was a founding member of the VFW post in Truckee, Calif.

"He was very, very patriotic," she said. "When our children were younger and they had no school for Memorial Day, Labor Day, Flag Day, Veterans Day, whatever it was - we always went to the cemeteries, we always saw the parades. They knew what those holidays were for."

Their children, Eric, Joe, 26, and Sierra, 25, are supportive of Wilkison's trip.

"They know it's something I need to do, and they think it will be a good healing time for me," she said.

Wilkison will have her cell phone and laptop to document her journey. Keep tabs on where she is over the summer at her website, annieamerika2012.blogspot.com, or at facebook.com/AnnieAmerika2012.

Gale Wilkison of Bridgeport holds the folded American flag given to her after her husband's funeral in 2010. Photo by Jennifer Marshall

June 11, 2012
"Annie Amerika stops in Spokane, traveling country replacing old flags"
By Othello Richards and *KREM.com*

SPOKANE - A north central Washington woman has set out on a 9,000 mile journey around the country to replace worn and tattered American flags.

Monday she passed through Spokane County.

The woman left her hometown of Bridgeport, Washington Sunday. If you're flying a worn or tattered flag, she may just end up on your doorstep.

Gale is on a mission she says to spread patriotism throughout the country. On her 2 month journey she's using the name Annie Amerika.

Two years ago Annie's husband, a Vietnam veteran, retired. Annie say john talked about the two of them traveling the country, visiting family and national parks. Along the way he wanted to replace old and dilapidated flags they came across. In November of 2010, john was killed in a car accident

A year a half later, Annie has set out to fulfill his goal. "I'm doing this for him, but I'm also doing this to heal my heart. "

Sponsors donated flags and money towards the cause. Annie started her trip with 81 flags to give away; at least one for each day on the road.

Annie's journey will take her to the east coast, where she plans to leave a picture of john at the Vietnam memorial in D.C. She then will head towards the gulf coast, and onto the pacific before she arrives back home in Bridgeport.

Annie gives old flags she receives to Boy Scout troops so they can properly retire them.

Comments

Melissa: That is so cool Gale! What a story and a true act of patriotism! You do America proud! Safe travels!
Jennifer: So cool!!
Karen: Thank you. Be Safe in your travels. You are an Angel
Sandra: Krem 2 did an awesome job of sharing your story!
Angie: Happy Trails to you.....until...we meet....again!!
Cathy: Safe travels. I pray you will meet many wonderful people on your journey and make many new friends all across the nation.
Jax: I just saw your story tonight on the news and wanted to say Thank You!!! Prayers for a safe journey!!
Lois: I am very impressed with your story; it is so nice to see someone concerned about the flags that are getting worn out. To be able to fulfill the dream of your husband is so touching, God Bless, be safe.

June 14, 2012
"Annie Amerika stops in Valley"
The Independent
By Kellie Trudeau

Gale Wilkison presents a new flag to Barbara and Stacy "Hoss" Murray at their home in Valley. Sandra Fish photo

Gale Wilkison, who calls herself "Annie Amerika," stopped in Valley on June 10 to present a new American flag to homeowners Barbara and Stacy "Hoss" Murray. It was the second day of Wilkison's two-month road trip across the country to promote patriotism in honor of her late husband.

Wilkison will travel nearly 9,000 miles on a round trip journey through the back roads of 27 states to replace worn flags as a free gift to unsuspecting patriots. It is a trip her husband, John, a disabled Vietnam Naval Veteran, had dreamed of taking before he was killed in a single vehicle accident in November 2010. They had been together for 30 years.

She is taking the trip on her own to "honor my husband, our country, its veterans, and to help heal my heart," Wilkison shares with everyone on her Internet blog.

Wilkison said her husband is the most patriotic person she has ever known. The first thing he always did was put the flagpole up outside every residence they rented or owned and took it down every night if it was not lit. It became a family ritual.

She plans to scout out worn flags as she travels and offer the owner, whom she will not know, a replacement. Wilkison has 81 flags with her and hopes to give at least one away each day.

The Murrays' property was the third stop for Wilkison who began the journey on June 9 in her hometown of Bridgeport, Wash.

Since ITD Productions of Valley sponsored the flag that Wilkison presented to the Murrays, she planned the stop for June 10 on her way from Bridgeport to Cheney. Teresa Nelson of ITD Productions, a friend of Wilkison, had previously spotted the Murrays' flagpole placed prominently in the center of their front lawn and said she saw that the flag was a "perfect" candidate for the project as it was in poor condition. ITD Productions has donated many other flags as well.

Barbara Murray said their flagpole was given to them as wedding gift from a friend when they were married on Sept. 21, 2001, just ten days after the 9/11 attacks. She said they are honored to be a part of the "Annie Amerika" route, especially since they had just been talking about their need for a new flag since it was faded and severely tattered on the edges.

Trying to hold back tears, Wilkison presented the new flag to the Murrays by saying: "On behalf of my husband John, I would like you to accept this flag to fly proudly at your home."

Boy Scouts of Troop 989 of Valley took down the old flag and raised the new flag. The Troop then held a flag retirement ceremony to burn the three worn flags that Wilkison had collected on her journey thus far.

The retirement ceremony, which took place in the Murrays' backyard, was an emotional one for Wilkison as she knew how proud her husband would have been to see it. He was a Boy Scout in his youth.

"They did a fantastic job, it is exactly what John would have wanted," Wilkison said. "He wanted to make sure future generations knew how to retire flags properly."

Wilkison had always planned to donate worn flags to Boy Scout troops along the journey once she collected eight or ten, but said this is probably the only retirement ceremony she will actually witness on the entire trip.

Troop 989 Scoutmaster Tim Thompson presented the charred flag grommets to Wilkison out of the fire following the ceremony. He also found one that was not charred, which he said was very unusual. She plans to put it on her key chain.

On her trip, Wilkison said she will visit three large bodies of water from the Atlantic Ocean, to the Gulf of Mexico to Astoria, Oregon on the Pacific Coast. She is traveling in a 1985 Chevrolet Campervan that she purchased in 2011.

Kimberly Gormley at Signs Etcetera of Waterville, Wash. painted the van in a patriotic theme that makes a statement to anyone who sees it. Major sponsors for "Annie Amerika" are listed in the stars of the large bright design. These include the VFW, of which John was a lifetime member among many other groups and individuals. Wilkison said she has been amazed by all the people who have offered their support.

Wilkison said all the flags are from Annin Flagmakers, which are American-made and have been used in every presidential inauguration since Abraham Lincoln except for the most recent one for Barack Obama.

Follow Wilkison on her trip at www.annieamerika2012.blogspot.com or at www.facebook.com/annieamerika2012. Wilkison said she did not misspell America as any disrespect to the country, but as a way to create a unique online identity.

June 28, 2012
"State of Washington Vietnam vet's widow visited Argyle on cross country memorial trip"
Pecatonica Valley Leader
Argyle/Blanchardville/Hollandale

Argyle received a special visitor late last week, from Annie Amerika, a Bridgeport, Washington resident who is traveling across the nation in memory of her late husband and Vietnam War veteran, John E. Wilkison.

"I've been traveling since June 10 and a cross country trip is something that my husband and I had always talked about doing," said Amerika, in a brief stop in her colorful van, at the Pec Valley Leader office on State Street, "Over the past 30 years that John and I have been together, we have noticed many worn American flags flying, and wanted to take pride in replacing them... with new flags. We also talked about donating the retired flags to local Boy Scout troops so they could learn how to properly retire them."

"We sold our 1979 Ford Campervan and bought a classic Superior motorhome, and we named her Ginger, in preparation for this once-in-a-lifetime trip. John was the most patriotic man I have ever met; he was proud to be an American and having served in the Navy."

But, back on November 7, 2000, John was tragically killed in a single vehicle accident, and my life was turned upside down. I had to sell Ginger and the hopes of traveling across America with the man I love. As time went on, I realized that this trip was extremely important to me as it was to John. I bought a 1985 Chevy Campervan and started planning my trip for the summer of 2012.

"Our children knew, while growing up, that on holidays like Memorial Day, the Fourth of July and Veterans Day, we were the sort of folks who visited cemeteries and always paid tribute to fallen servicemen, to military veterans and to the red, white and blue. My husband and I spent 30 wonderful years together – and I decided that I was going to make this journey on my own, even without him. My plan is to cross the nation, to be at the Vietnam Veterans Memorial in Washington D.C. on July 4, to continue on to the Atlantic, then cut southwesterly towards the Gulf of Mexico and I will head back up to Astoria, Oregon to end my journey in mid-August."

I left Washington with 81 flags and since I'm a small-town girl at heart, I'm taking the back roads across America, and taking my time, and once a day as I'm traveling through a different town, I look for a flag that's perhaps a little bit old and worn – and I stop and give a new flag to the folks who live in the home or house. I came through Argyle today – where I had a nice visit and left a flag with a woman (Audrey Wilhelmson, a Lafayette Street resident) who was spending time taking care of her grandchildren."

"I've received a wonderful response from wonderful people all along my journey and I am staying in state parks and in parking lots as I make the trip as economically feasible as possible. I always say the Pledge of Allegiance with whomever I give the new flag to and I have taken the old flags and I'm donating those to the Boy Scouts for proper retirement."

"In one town, in fact, they (the local Boy Scout unit) held a flag retirement ceremony with me as their guest – which of course was an honor as well."

Amerika headed out of Argyle Wednesday afternoon, departing for the border town of Antioch, Illinois a community where her father lives and where she planned to spend two days before heading eastward.

The following comments – on her Argyle visit are via Annie's daily blog posted Wednesday evening:

'I slept very well last night (at Blue Mounds State Park) considering the raccoons woke me up twice. You see, I had left my basil plant outside and they 'played in the dirt,' didn't eat the basil though... I then headed east on Hwy 18 and before I knew it I was at the Cave of the Mounds Park.

'I had missed my turn off headed south – but while there I met a young dad and his two small children; they liked my colorful van. I gave the children a small handheld American Flag and it made me smile. I headed south and found myself in Argyle. Have you been here? If you had, you would remember this town and its people. I had been driving up and down the streets for a while when I found Audrey; she was taking care of her grandchildren, and they needed a flag. We talked some and I gave the two children each a hand-held American flag. They said the Pledge of Allegiance with me, and I took a photo of the children in front of the new flag. What I want you to know about Audrey is that her handshake was strong, she looked me in the eyes and thanked me, and it was a special moment. Thank you – Audrey!'"

June 28, 2012
The Morning Journal
"Woman travels across country to replace tattered American flags"
By Jason Henry

LORAIN – Gale Wilkison's husband, John, was the most patriotic man she ever met and after his death in 2010, Wilkison decided to honor him and help herself through the grief process by finding and replacing worn or tattered U.S. flags in communities across the United States.

The 9,000-mile trip had been planned in the summer of 2010 by the couple, but John's sudden death in a car accident the following fall halted the idea until Wilkison, a teacher's aide, started the trip from her hometown of Bridgeport, Wash., on June 10.

"He died just a few months after we talked about it," she said. "For the first year, there was a lot of adjustment, a lot of changes, and then I decided, 'You know what, John wanted to do this trip. I'm going to do it for him. I'm going to do it on his behalf.'"

Wilkison, under the mantle of "Annie Amerika," landed in Lorain County last week, to continue spreading her message.

"I was given the nickname 'Annie' a little over a year ago and I decided that instead of taking the trip with my real name, Gale Wilkison, I was going to do it under Annie Amerika, because it isn't about me, it is about John and his patriotism and his wish to do this," she said.

John viewed damaged flags as disrespectful and wanted to help out other patriotic people who needed replacements.

"John was a Vietnam veteran and he had a problem with worn and tattered flags," she said. "He just wanted to replace the worn or tattered flags of unsuspecting homeowners along the way."

Wilkison decided to complete the trip the way her husband would want to do it — with little planning.

"I'm a planner, if I did it my way, I would plan out everything," she said. "It's not my trip, it is John's trip. John was very spontaneous. I'm doing it John's way."

She felt that the trip would give her a chance to complete the task of which her husband dreamed. It also would act as a kind of therapy for her after the loss of her husband of 30 years.

"This is part of the reason I'm doing the trip," she said. "I need to be able to talk about it without crying, I need to heal. And I'm hoping this will help me."

Besides certain goals created by John, such as being at the Vietnam Veteran's Memorial in Washington, D.C., on the Fourth of July, Wilkison has awaken every morning, looked at a map and plotted her course for that day.

She scheduled only five hotel reservations for the entire 90-day trip.

The method of travel also stays strict to John's ideals. Wilkison avoids interstates whenever she can, sticking to back roads and two-lane highways which run through small communities.

The decision adds quite a few miles to her trip.

With 81 flags — for 15 to 25 foot flag poles — Wilkison had dispersed roughly one-a-day during her trip. She had given away 24 by last week, three of which went to Ohioans.

Wilkison said she typically waits until the mid-afternoon and then drives through a community searching for a home with a worn flag. She then goes to the door and presents the owners with a new one and collects the old flags to donate to Boy Scout troops to help them learn to dispose properly of flags.

Meeting new people has been the highlight of the trip.

In Northern Illinois, a local Boy Scout troop tipped Wilkison off about a veteran's homecoming party.

"I'd never been to a homecoming, all I knew was what John told me about how they treated him when he got back from Vietnam and people were not nice to him," she said. "It was really overwhelming because everyone just embraced him and treated him so well."

She gave the just returned veteran one of her flags.

"It was good to see he had a hero's welcome, like he should," she said.

Wilkison is making the trip in 1985 Chevy Campervan decorated with patriotic imagery and the names of her sponsors. She hasn't been alone, however, as she has a constant companion in Charlie, a tomato plant perched on her passenger seat.

"He is the perfect companion because he doesn't care where I stop or when I stop," she said with a laugh.

The older vehicle hasn't always cooperated. She has had a few breakdowns during the trip. In Wyoming, her water pump, thermostat, fan clutch and radiator cap had to be replaced. Earlier last week, she noticed a chunk of her tire missing and her non-standard back tires required four new tires to be bought so all four would match up.

Later in the week, a vacuum hose came off her PCV valve. All of the mechanics have been helpful and supportive of her cause, but workers at a Lube Stop in Avon Lake went beyond the call and replaced the hose for free.

After a stop in Geneva on the Lake, where John grew up, Wilkison will make her way to Washington, D.C. She plans to eventually hit the Atlantic, then head down to the gulf of Mexico — particularly looking forward to a stop in Graceland — and then she plans to loop back to the Pacific.

Though she only had 81 flags to give out, she said she'd consider expanding the trip longer if more were donated.

"I've always been a strong-willed, independent person, so doing the trip has been fun," she said. "I love meeting new people. I love getting to see new towns."

For those interested in following Wilkison's trip, visit www.annieamerika2012.blogspot.com or www.facebook.com/annieamerika2012.

Comments

Elizabeth: great article
Bambi: You did a great job and you didn't even seem nervous!!!
Lisa: Very touching

July 5, 2012
KREM 2 News
"'Annie Amerika' honors late husband at Vietnam memorial"

SPOKANE – This Fourth of July was very special for a Washington woman. She's fulfilling her quest to honor her husband and the heroes of our country.

We introduced you to Annie Amerika back in June. She's traveling around the country replacing tattered flags in her husband's honor.

We spoke to her Wednesday about how her trip is going. Gale Wilkison started her trip in Washington. She has a batch of new flags to replace old. So far she's replaced more than 30.

Another part of her mission is for her late husband John, a Vietnam vet. She wanted to make it to the Vietnam veteran's memorial in Washington, D.C.

On the 4th she laid his picture alongside a friend's at the wall. She says the trip has connected her to proud Americans around the country.

She's not done with her trip. She has more flags to give away and is expecting to come home in August.

Comments

Pat: So proud of you, John is also smiling on you. Stay safe.

July 15, 2012
News 14 Carolina
"'Annie Amerika' driving across the US to replace tattered flags"
By David Kernodle

MATTHEWS, N.C. - A Washington woman is on a patriotic pilgrimage.

Gale Wilkison, who goes by the name 'Annie Amerika,' is driving across the country replacing tattered flags.

She was in the Charlotte area Wednesday afternoon, and News 14 Carolina reporter David Kernodle caught up with her and found out why she's doing it.

July 20, 2012
WKRG News 5
Mobile, Alabama
"Woman Makes Cross-Country Journey"
By Devon Walsh

A woman from Washington State is in Alabama, on a cross-country mission to carry out her late husband's mission. She is going by the name "Annie Amerika" as a way to show how she is proud to be an American.

She stops in small towns, knocks on doors, and offers to replace torn flags with new ones. She has never been turned down.

Gale is travelling 9,000 miles across the country in her van to honor her late husband, John's memory. He was a disabled Vietnam Veteran, who died in a car accident a year and a half ago.

She says, "Part of the reason for the trip was not only to fulfill John's wishes and fulfill his bucket list with an old-fashioned America road trip, but it was also healing for me."

Gale takes the tattered flags she's collected, and meets with Boy Scout troops along the way, for a flag retirement ceremony. News Five was there when she shared her story with Spanish Fort Troop 177. She gave them 34 flags to properly dispose of. They held a flag-burning ceremony. The boys say the ceremony was very meaningful.

Keaton Morris says, "This one felt like it had a greater cause, than anything else. It felt like we were doing this for somebody or something."

Troop leader, Brian Brey says, "It shows the compassion and the drive to keep something that was near and dear to her heart."

Gale, or "Annie Amerika," was very touched by the ceremony. She has 3,000 miles left on her journey.

ABOUT THE AUTHOR

Annie is the proud widow of a disabled Vietnam Veteran. She works in a public school teaching students in North Central Washington. In her free time she enjoys camping with her children and her amazing grandchildren, Alex, Tessa-Lynn and Maddie.

Made in the USA
Charleston, SC
03 June 2014